Computer and Internet Use on Campus

Computer and Internet Use on Campus

A Legal Guide to Issues of Intellectual Property, Free Speech, and Privacy

Constance S. Hawke

JOSSEY-BASS
A Wiley Company
San Francisco

Jossey-Bass Books and products are available through most bookstores. To contact Jossey-Bass directly, call (888) 378-2537, fax to (800) 605-2665, or visit our website at www.josseybass.com.

Substantial discounts on bulk quantities of Jossey-Bass books are available to corporations, professional associations, and other organizations. For details and discount information, contact the special sales department at Jossey-Bass.

Printed in the United States of America.

Library of Congress Cataloging-in-Publication Data

Hawke, Constance S., 1952–
    Computer and internet use on campus: a legal guide to issues of intellectual property, free speech, and privacy/
Constance S. Hawke—1st ed.
        p.   cm. —(The Jossey-Bass higher and adult education series)
Includes bibliographical reference and index.
        ISBN 0-7879-5516-7 (alk. paper)
        1. Computer networks—Law and legislation—United States.   2. Computers—Law and legislation—United States.   3. College students—Legal status, laws, etc.—United States.   4. Internet (Computer network)   I. Title.   II. Series.
KF390.5.C6 H39   2001
343.7309'944—dc21

PB Printing   10 9 8 7 6 5 4 3 2 1   FIRST EDITION

The Jossey-Bass
Higher and Adult Education Series

Contents

To my children:
Lindsay, Kyle, Ashley, and Kelsey—
you are, by God's grace, my magnum opus.

The Author

Constance S. Hawke is the special assistant to the president for federal relations at Kent State University, where she also has taught undergraduate and graduate classes in business and education law. She has been a practicing attorney for more than twenty years and is a member of the Ohio and Florida bars.

She earned a B.A. in psychology from Bowling Green State University (1974); a J.D. from Cleveland Marshall College of Law (1977); and a Ph.D. in educational administration from Kent State University (1999). She has published articles concerning education and employment law.

Introduction

The advent of the computer age has bridged any gap that may have existed between college life and life in the outside world. Advancements in communications technology have had pervasive effects on higher education, allowing a previously sheltered student population instantaneous global connections to the rest of the world without leaving campus, the residence hall, or even home.

Today, most major colleges and universities have technology infrastructures in place and are providing some on-line services for their students, educators, and administrators. A recent survey of more than one hundred higher education institutions considered to be among the "most wired" nationwide indicates that almost all provide students with unlimited Internet access, e-mail, and even space for personal home pages. Moreover, distance learning via the Web is being offered with increasing frequency. Notwithstanding the philosophical debates that may ensue over such a transformation of higher education, it is indisputable that technology has arrived on American campuses and may become a measure of an institution's success in the future.

Introducing computer technology on college and university campuses has required institutions to undertake multiple initiatives: providing the infrastructure for computer use on campus (i.e., the hardware, wiring, cables, switches that run the system); hiring technological support to keep the system operating; and offering training for students, faculty, and staff. Colleges and universities generally provide Internet access through the campus network at no charge to the university community, although a growing number of institutions are charging a technology fee to students to defray costs attributable to computer networks. In providing such access, higher education institutions have taken on an entirely new role as Internet service providers.

There is also evidence that campus networks, and particularly the Internet, are becoming important components of the curriculum. The majority of colleges and universities in the United States provide access for their students and faculty either through direct connection using computers located in campus libraries or computer centers, or through telephone access using a modem from the individual's on-campus or off-campus location. Many institutions are installing ports in residence halls to provide direct in-room access to the campus network, enabling students to use information provided by the university itself as well as the vast amount of information on the Internet.

By inviting the Internet to college campuses, institutions of higher education may have opened new vistas of opportunity for research and communication for the university community. Advocates purport that cyberspace is a new frontier for unmonitored, and therefore uncensored, communication and the free exchange of ideas. But the Internet has its dark side as well, affording an opportunity and anonymity for those who choose to use the electronic environment for immoral, unethical, and even illegal purposes. As the Internet service provider for students and employees, colleges and universities must be concerned with these problems, not only for the greater good of the university community but because an institution itself may incur potential civil liability for abuses that occur over its network. At the same time, however, the institution must balance the interests of the university community to receive and disseminate information freely and to afford protection for the rights of its constituents.

With the surge of computer technology on college campuses across the nation, incidents of abuse of campus networks are becoming more prevalent, resulting in both criminal and civil litigation. Among the incidents in recent years that have been reported or that resulted in lawsuits are the following:

In 1995, a student at the University of Michigan was expelled from the university and faced criminal charges for posting a fantasy rape story about one of his classmates to a sex story newsgroup.

In 1996, a student at California State University-Northridge used his home page created on the university's computer system to politically attack the incumbent in a state senate race, including a photograph of the candidate that transformed into a skeleton as the viewer watched.

At Northwestern University, a professor published a university-sponsored home page in which he espoused the view that the Holocaust was a hoax.

In 1997, a University of Oklahoma professor filed a lawsuit protesting university restrictions on student access to certain newsgroups.

At California State University, forty-two professors with Hispanic surnames received racist and threatening e-mail messages.

A student at the University of California was prosecuted for sending sixty e-mail messages to Asian American students and staff members in which he threatened to kill them.

University concerns are not limited to abuses by and against students. Employees have been the target of the following terminations:

At East Tennessee State University, an administrator was fired when an audit revealed that he used his university computer to visit adult entertainment sites on the Web.

At the University of Alaska, a university carpenter was fired after a new tracking system alerted administrators that he was visiting child pornography sites from his university computer.

At the University of West Florida, an employee was fired for down-loading child pornography while on the job.

Universities are also faced with equally important issues relating to the use of intellectual property and the possibility of copyright or trademark infringement. For example, in a recent incident, a university disciplined more than seventy students who were caught distributing illegally copied MP3 audio files on the campus network. MP3s are audio files on the Internet that may be downloaded by computer user or sent to other users. While some MP3 sites are authorized, other sites allow users to download songs or albums without paying for them and are in violation of copyright laws.

The introduction of the computer network and the Internet on campus has opened a labyrinth of legal issues for higher education. An awareness of the legal ramifications of Internet activity by the university community can help maximize use and minimize risk of litigation for individual users as well as the institution. It is particularly important for institutions already confronted with a scarcity of financial resources to avoid wasting them defending litigation that could have been avoided by proactive planning and education of the university community.

The focus of this book is on the legal issues and policy concerns that arise from providing computer networks on campus. Higher education may be a unique environment in some respects, but it is a microcosm of society in others. Consequently, the issues identified are not limited to higher education; concerns about intellectual property, freedom of speech, and privacy extend to Internet providers and users off campus as well.

The popularity of Internet use for personal, commercial, and educational uses has catapulted the legal parameters of its use to the forefront for legislatures and courts. In their respective legislative and judicial roles, each must grapple with the extent to which existing laws, when applied to this relatively new environment of cyberspace, have fair and desirable results.

Technological advances have spawned new forms of media over the past century, from broadcasting to cable television and now to computer networks. Each of these technologies has brought with it challenges and problems that require courts and legislatures to review existing laws to determine if they can be applied to the new forms of media or if they require reconfiguration.

The adaptation of law to technology is not a new phenomenon. When technological advances produced telephone wiretapping capabilities earlier this century, the Supreme Court ruled that wiretapping did not constitute unreasonable search and seizure because there was no actual or physical intrusion in the defendant's house (Olmstead v. United States, 277 U.S. 438 (1928)). It was almost forty years later that the Court reversed its position that another's voice spoken into a telephone receiver did constitute a search under the Fourth Amendment. The fact that there was no physical intrusion was no longer relevant in light of the ability to carry out a technological "invasion" (Katz v. United States, 389 U.S. 347 (1967)).

Similarly, the birth of broadcasting, in which technology allowed the delivery of audio and video programming over airwaves to multiple receivers within range of a signal brought about a change in the level of First Amendment protections afforded free speech. Although the courts traditionally have been loathe to permit any government regulation of speech for written materials, the scarcity of frequencies over which to transmit broadcasts and the pervasiveness of the broadcast medium have resulted in the Supreme Court's upholding content-based regulation of broadcasters' speech (see FCC v. Pacifica Foundation, 438 U.S. 726 (1978)).

The foregoing examples illustrate instances in which the Supreme Court found it necessary to adapt a legal paradigm to the new technology, which does not necessarily imply that all existing laws must be rewritten for the computer network environment. To the contrary, the judiciary will make every effort to apply existing legal precedent to cases arising out of activity on the Internet under the rule of *stare decisis* that governs American jurisprudence. What is warranted is a careful examination of the current constitutional, statutory, and common law in order to anticipate how the courts will decide cases that may arise out of Internet use.

How these issues of law and technology are resolved is of great importance to higher education. Regulation of the broader Internet environment has an impact on university participation and use and will ultimately determine if institutional investment in computer networks was prudent. Given the apparent magnitude of that investment, institutions of higher education may want to have a voice in the future of cyberspace.

The purpose of this book is threefold: to inform users of the legal ramifications of their on-line activities; to help administrators handle specific situations or complaints regarding Internet activity; and to provide guidance for the formulation of acceptable computer use policies on campuses. It may serve as a starting point for attorneys and administrators confronted with abuses of the campus network and a reference for students, faculty, and staff who want to be informed users of that network. Student affairs officials also need to understand the legal framework for dealing with infractions by students. Furthermore, the rapid growth of distance learning and the attendant issues of faculty ownership make this book a valuable resource for academic administrators. In the following chapters, four main legal issues are identified and discussed. A set of specific recommendations for network use on campus concludes each chapter.

Chapter One explores intellectual property issues. Traditional protections afforded copyrights and trademarks have become complicated in the electronic environment, and ownership of on-line course materials has become an issue on many campuses.

Chapter Two examines an old problem in a new context: the delicate balance between free speech and the protection of individuals from defamation, obscenity, and harassment. The context is now cyberspace, which is currently free from government regulation and where anonymity of the sender is possible.

Chapter Three focuses on privacy issues that have become a major source of concern for users of the information superhighway. Given the increasing amount of information available and the growing proficiency of the population to access it, there is greater potential for litigation emanating from violations of privacy interests. In addition, institutions of higher education must maintain security for informational privacy of their students and understand the legal limitations imposed on the administration of campus networks.

Chapter Four addresses issues of due process and fairness in the computer network arena. Communications on the Internet travel across state and national boundaries almost instantaneously; consequently, legal jurisdictional concepts that depend on a geographical nexus are problematic in lawsuits arising out of computer network use.

Finally, a checklist of policy recommendations and guidelines for system administrators is provided to assist higher education institutions in educating its users and preventing future abuses.

One caveat exists: this book serves only as a legal guide to campus network use and should not be used as a substitute for the advice of informed legal counsel. Creation of universal policies should be done in conjunction with counsel who understand the unique culture of the institution and have a sense of what would maximize use of the system while at the same time minimizing the legal risk to the institution. Moreover, ongoing consultation with counsel is important while the legal landscape of computer and Internet use continues to unfold, both in the legislatures and in the courtroom.

1

Intellectual Property On-Line

R esearch and scholarship are perhaps the sine qua non of higher education. As a result, colleges and universities are bastions for the intellectual property that is a product of these pursuits. At the same time, access to the intellectual property created by others is an essential element of learning in higher education. Because it is such an important factor in higher education, it is not surprising that issues surrounding the protection and use of intellectual property in the electronic forum are of particular concern on college and university campuses.

We have the technology now to digitize and disseminate intellectual property globally. The Internet provides an easy and inexpensive way to reach a large audience, which may be advantageous for authors who wish to distribute their work directly to a large number of consumers. Publishing on the Web is a relatively simple matter for prospective authors, requiring only a personal computer, appropriate software, and a modem (*see* ACLU v. Reno, 929 F. Supp. 824, 837 (E.D. Pa. 1996), *cert. granted*, 117 S. Ct. 554 (1996), *aff'd*, 117 S. Ct. 2329 (1997)).

Although cyberspace offers a new venue for the innovative to disseminate their work, there is no assurance that the creator will reap its benefits. In fact, the increasing availability of digitized intellectual property, coupled with the soaring use of the Internet, sets the stage for massive copyright infringement. Distribution of a work on the Internet allows uncontrolled copying or modification by any number of users. Copyrighted works in digital form may be instantaneously transmitted to hundreds or thousands of subscribers who, in turn, may download or print unlimited copies without paying a royalty to the copyright owner. Not only may a user deliver perfect copies of a digitized work by a few keystrokes on a computer, but digitization also allows a work easily to be altered or mutilated, further infringing on the rights of the copyright holder.

As a result of this higher risk of unauthorized use, some fear that reputable authors and scholars may be reluctant to digitize their work. Even if authors choose not to digitize their works for the Internet market, the risk is not completely eliminated. One unauthorized uploading of a work to the Internet, unlike most single reproductions in the print environment, may have devastating effects on the market for the work. In addition to this technological vulnerability of copyrighted works, there appears to be a developing Internet attitude or culture that promotes unrestricted use of anything available on the Internet. The tension between ownership rights and the right to access information has been the subject of debate for several years.

Although the right to access and use digitized works remains controversial, administrators of campus computer networks are faced with applying existing laws to incidents occurring on campus networks. Administrators may be faced for the first time with students downloading MP3s from the Internet or graduate students downloading graphics from the Internet and including them in their dissertation. An administrator also may be confronted with situations in which a faculty member posts copyrighted material for students to use in an on-line course. Understanding the legal implications of these activities helps to develop policy and practices that educate users and protect the institution from liability.

Statutory Framework

Although copyright legislation has been in place since 1790, current copyright controversies are resolved under the Copyright Act of 1976 (hereafter referred to as the Act), which was amended in part in 1998 to address computer technology issues. The following sections provide an overview of the nature and scope of copyright protection afforded by current laws.

Eligibility for Protection

Under section 102(a) of the Act, copyright protection extends to original works of authorship fixed in any tangible medium of expression, now known or later developed, from which they can be "perceived, reproduced, or otherwise communicated, either directly or with the aid of a machine or device." Copyright protection extends to the *expression* of ideas, procedures, and concepts only, not to the ideas, procedures, or concepts themselves, which may be used by anyone. The courts have determined that the following are required for eligibility under the Act: the work must be original (i.e., an independent creation not copied from another work); creative (i.e., even a slight amount is sufficient); and fixed (i.e., when the embodiment of the work in a copy is permanent or stable enough to permit it to be perceived, reproduced, or communicated).

The Act enumerates eight categories of subject matter that fall under copyright protection: literary works; musical works; dramatic works; pantomimes and choreographic works; pictorial, graphic, and sculptural works; motion pictures and audiovisual works; sound recordings; and architectural works. The majority of works available on computer networks would fall within the first category of "literary works," which are expressed in "words, numbers, or other verbal or numerical indicia, regardless of the nature of the material objects, such as books, periodicals, manuscripts, phonorecords, films, tapes, disks, or cards, in which they are embodied" (17 U.S.C. § 101

(1998)). Under this definition, digitized original works are entitled to copyright protection.

Copyright Ownership

The determination of ownership is crucial in establishing who holds the copyright to a particular work. The Act states that copyright ownership in a work initially vests in the author of the work (17 U.S.C. § 201(a) (1998)). Generally, work created by two or more authors is a joint work and the authors are considered co-owners of the copyright in the work (17 U.S.C. § 201(b) (1998)). In addition, there are two types of works-for-hire according to the Act: those prepared by an employee and those prepared by an independent contractor by special order or commission. Although the Act does not specifically define employee, it does state that the copyright in a work prepared by an employee within the scope of employment vests in the employer and the employer is the author (17 U.S.C. § 101 (1998)).

Copyright ownership—as distinguished from ownership of a copy of a work—entitles the copyright owner to exercise certain exclusive rights, whereas ownership of a copy (i.e., a book, CD, videocassette) carries with it no interest in the copyright.

Section 106 of the Act grants the copyright owner these exclusive rights:

1. To reproduce the copyrighted work in copies or phonorecords

2. To prepare derivative works based on the copyrighted work

3. To distribute copies or phonorecords of the copyrighted work to the public by sale or other transfer of ownership, or by rental, lease, or lending

4. In the case of literary, musical, dramatic, and choreographic works, pantomimes, and motion pictures and other audiovisual works, to perform the copyrighted work publicly

5. In the case of literary, musical, dramatic, and choreographic works, pantomimes and pictorial, graphic or sculptural works,

including the individual images of a motion picture or other audiovisual work, to display the copyrighted work publicly

6. In the case of sound recordings, to perform the copyrighted work publicly by a means of a digital audio transmission

The exclusive right to reproduce the work is implicated in most computer-to-computer communications that are fundamental to Internet use. Any time a computer user accesses a document that resides on another computer, the user's computer reproduces or copies the document in its memory, thereby allowing the image to exist on the user's screen. The courts have repeatedly held that placing a work in computer memory (whether by scanning or digitizing or by uploading or downloading to another server) creates a copy or reproduction of the work. Without such copying into memory, no screen display would be possible (see MAI Sys. Corp. v. Peak Computer, 991 F.2d 511 (9th Cir. 1993), cert. denied, 114 S. Ct. 671 (1994); Vault Corp. v. Quaid Software, 847 F.2d 255 (5th Cir. 1988); Advanced Computer Sys. v. MAI Sys. Corp., 845 F. Supp. (E.D. Va. 1994)).

The right to prepare derivative works grants copyright owners the right to control revisions, adaptations, and other "transformations" of their work. Thus, any modification by a user of a downloaded file could constitute a derivative work in violation of the owner's exclusive right. Similarly, the right to distribute copies gives the copyright holder the right to authorize or prohibit the initial distribution of a copy of a copyrighted work (although a subsequent owner may sell or dispose of that copy). However, a user who makes copies without authorization and distributes them may be liable for infringement of the right to distribute.

According to the Act, the right to publicly perform a work is limited to owners of literary, musical, dramatic, and choreographic works, pantomimes, motion pictures, and other audiovisual works. Only public performances (those open to the public or where a substantial number of people are gathered, excluding a small number of family members and social acquaintances) are protected under the Act. Some commentators have speculated that the definition of public may be construed by the courts to include performances or displays over the Internet where many individuals may view the work from diverse locations.

The fifth exclusive right gives the owner the right to display a work publicly. Under the Act, to display a work means to show a copy of it, either directly or by means of any other device or process. Based on the foregoing definition, any copyrighted work posted to the Internet that is visually browsed by another user would constitute a public display of the work.

The last exclusive right is limited to the right to duplicate the sound recording and does not include any right of performance. Consequently, the performance of a sound recording publicly by means of a digital audio transmission does not infringe on the owners exclusive rights, provided that the performance is part of a nonsubscription broadcast transmission or retransmission (17 U.S.C. § 114)(1999)).

In addition to the grant of exclusive rights, the Act gives the copyright owner the ability to authorize or to prevent others from exercising any of the exclusive rights. Ownership of a copyright or any of the exclusive rights of ownership may be transferred to one or more persons, provided that the transfer is in writing and signed by the transferor. A transfer of copyright ownership may be limited in some respects (i.e., time or place), but it must be an exclusive transfer of the rights involved. A transfer of nonexclusive rights does not transfer ownership but grants a license to another person to use the copyrighted work while the copyright owner retains ownership. The copyright owner may grant similar licenses to others without the necessity of a written agreement. Where a written (or oral) agreement exists, the terms of the contract determine the use of the copyrighted work by the licensee that can be enforced under state law.

The term of protection for a copyrighted work is generally for the length of the author's life plus seventy years (17 U.S.C. § 302(a), as amended by the Copyright Term Extension Act of 1997, Pub. L. No. 105-298 (Oct. 27, 1998)). For joint works, the protection lasts until seventy years after the death of the last surviving joint author (17 U.S.C. § 302(b), as amended (1998)). In the case of works made for hire, anonymous and pseudonymous works, the protection lasts ninety-five years from the year of first publication or 120 years from the year of creation, whichever is shorter (17 U.S.C. § 302(c), as amended (1998)). After the expiration of a term of protection for a copyrighted work, the work falls into the public domain and may be used freely by the public. The Copyright Extension Act includes an exception that permits libraries and nonprofit educational institutions to treat a copyrighted work in the last twenty years of protection as if it were in the public domain as long as the intended use of the work is not commercial, and if the work is not currently being used in a commercial manner. Moreover, such use of the copyrighted work must stop if the copyright owner objects (17 U.S.C. § 108 (2000)).

Since 1989 the use of a copyright notice on publicly distributed copies from which the work can be perceived (either directly or with the aid of a machine or device) is permitted but not required. Although registration is not mandatory for the grant of exclusive rights, it is a prerequisite to the filing of a lawsuit for monetary damages (17 U.S.C. § 411(a) (1998)). This can be accomplished by filing a completed application, paying a registration fee, and providing the U.S. Copyright Office with a copy of the work. Removing notice and registration requirements provides authors with copyright protection without cumbersome filing requirements; however, the lack of mandatory notice on a protected work makes it more difficult, particularly in the computer network environment, to determine whether a work is protected or to ascertain the identity of the author and get permission to use it.

Direct Infringement

Under the Act, any unauthorized invasion of the exclusive rights of the copyright owner, without permission, constitutes infringement.

In order to prevail on a claim of direct copyright infringement, the plaintiff must prove ownership of the copyrighted work and that the defendant copied the work. The courts generally use the term *copying* when discussing a violation of any of the exclusive rights of the copyright owner, not just reproduction rights. When determining whether an infringement has occurred, the courts generally look at the "substantial similarity" of the protected expression of a copyrighted work and the "copy." In addition, the portion of the original work copied must be more than *de minimis* to constitute infringement (*see* Nimmer, 1993).

Direct copyright infringement does not require intent on the part of the infringing party; thus, even innocent or accidental infringement may be actionable. As a result, direct infringers are to be held to a standard of strict liability under the Act. However, the court does have the discretion to take into account the innocent or accidental nature of the infringement when awarding damages (17 U.S.C. § 504(c)(2) (1998)). Even though direct infringement carries with it the most stringent standard of liability, there is also the possibility of contributory and vicarious liability for infringement that provides additional protection for the copyright owner.

Contributory Liability

Although the Act does not define this term, case law has established that a person who has knowledge of the infringing activity, and who induces, causes, or materially contributes to the infringing conduct of another may be held contributorily liable (*see* Gershwin Pub'g Corp. v. Columbia Artists Management, 443 F.2d 1159 (2d Cir. 1971)). There is no prerequisite for direct participation in the infringing activity; hence, an individual or entity may be liable based solely on the provision of services or equipment used in the direct infringement. The concern therefore has been that a provider of a network computer system might be liable to copyright holders for unauthorized copying by its users.

The legal analysis for contributory infringement is more complex than for direct infringement. The courts are likely to find contributory infringement where there is (1) knowledge of the direct infringement and (2) the party induced, caused, or materially contributed to the conduct of the direct infringer. However, knowledge of the infringement requires more than an awareness that the infringement might occur; even an unsupported allegation of infringement may not be sufficient to put a defendant on notice of an infringing activity (*see* Religious Technology Center v. Netcom On-Line Communications Services, Inc., 907 F. Supp. 1361, 1374 (N.D. Cal. 1995)).

Vicarious Liability

The third theory of liability for infringing activity is vicarious liability. Under this theory, liability may be established, regardless of knowledge or lack of knowledge, where the party has (1) the right and ability to control the infringer's acts and (2) receives a direct financial benefit from the infringement. Thus, vicarious liability requires neither knowledge nor participation—it is based on the party's relationship to the direct infringer, not to the infringing activity itself.

Some early cases concerning on-line copyright infringement established that Internet service providers could be held liable for the infringing activities of their subscribers under theories of contributory or vicarious liability. In *Playboy Enterprises v. Frena*, 839 F. Supp. 1552 (M.D. Fla. 1993), defendant Frena operated a subscription bulletin board service (BBS) that distributed unauthorized copies of plaintiff's copyrighted photographs. Subscribers of defendant's service were able to log on to the BBS and browse through BBS directories, which included 170 copies of plaintiff's photographs. In addition, subscribers could download these photographs from the BBS and store them on their home computer. The defendant claimed that he did not upload the photographs to the BBS, and when he was made aware of their existence, he removed them from the BBS. After determining that plaintiff Playboy owned the copyright on the photographs and that the photographs on the BBS were substantially similar to the plaintiff's and were therefore copies within the definition of the Act, the court concluded that the exclusive display rights of the plaintiff had been violated. Moreover, the court found that the plaintiff's distribution rights were implicated when the defendant supplied the service (the BBS) containing unauthorized copies of a copyrighted work.

Similarly, in *Sega Enterprises Ltd.* v. *MAPHIA*, 857 F. Supp. 679 (N.D. Cal. 1994), a manufacturer and distributor of video games brought an action for copyright infringement against the operator of a bulletin board server. In that case, evidence established that Sega's copyrighted video games were uploaded to the MAPHIA bulletin board, where they could be downloaded in their entirety by an unlimited number of users. The BBS even advertised the availability of these games when one purchased a subscription to the BBS. The court granted a preliminary injunction against the operator of the bulletin board, finding that it was likely that the defendants would be held liable as contributory infringers, stating that "[e]ven if Defendants do not know exactly when games will be uploaded to or downloaded from the MAPHIA bulletin board, their role in the copying, including provision of facilities, direction, knowledge and encouragement, amounts to contributory copyright infringement" (*id.* at 687).

A 1995 decision of a federal district court in *Religious Technology Center* v. *Netcom On-Line Communications Services, Inc.*, 907 F. Supp. 1361 (N.D. Cal.1995), refused to extend liability to a service provider on a theory of direct infringement. The plaintiffs in that case held copyrights in the published and unpublished works of L. Ron Hubbard, the late founder of the Church of Scientology. One of the defendants, Erhlich, was a former minister of the Church of Scientology who had become a vocal critic of the religious organization. He posted portions of Hubbard's work to a Usenet newsgroup on-line forum for purposes of criticism. Erhlich gained access to the newsgroup through a small home-operated BBS, which in turn gained access to the Internet through the facilities of Netcom On-Line Communications Services, a large on-line access provider. After failing to convince Erhlich to stop his postings, the plaintiffs contacted the BBS operator and Netcom and asked them to deny Erhlich access to the Internet; those requests were denied by the respective defendants. Thereafter, the plaintiffs filed suit against Erhlich for copyright infringement and against the BBS and Netcom on the theories of direct, contributory, and vicarious liability. The court held that although it was likely Erhlich was liable for direct infringement, Netcom could not be a direct copyright infringer as a matter of law. The court also dismissed the claim based on vicarious liability. It did conclude, however, that Netcom could be liable on a theory of contributory liability because it allowed distribution of infringing material over its system and did not take steps to prevent further damage.

Several courts subsequently followed the analysis of the Netcom court. For example, in *Marobie-FL, Inc. v. National Association of Fire Equipment Distributors*, 983 F. Supp. 1167, (N.D. Ill. 1997), the court found that a service provider was not liable for direct and vicarious copyright infringement but may be held contributorily liable for copyrighted clip-art that was posted to the Internet through its service; in *Playboy Enterprises v. Russ Hardenbaugh, Inc.*, 982 F. Supp. 503, (N.D. Ohio 1997), the court held an access provider liable for direct and contributory copyright infringement on the basis that its screening to avoid pornography constituted substantial participation. These conflicting court decisions raised serious liability concerns for Internet service providers that were ultimately addressed in federal legislation.

Digital Millennium Copyright Act

In October 1998, the Digital Millennium Copyright Act of 1998 (DMCA) was signed into law, implementing two international copyright treaties and limiting liability for on-line copyright infringement, among other things. Title II of the DMCA creates a new section 512 of the Copyright Act whose provisions are relevant to education and research institutions. Popularly known as the Online Copyright Infringement Liability Limitation Act (OCILLA), 17 U.S.C §§ 512 *et seq.* (1998), section 512 limits liability for copyright infringement for on-line or Internet service providers; provides "safe harbor" liability limitations for system caching; establishes notice (and counternotice) provisions as part of liability limitation; and establishes special liability limitations for nonprofit educational institutions.

Provided prescribed conditions are met, service providers are immune from liability for infringement of a copyright by a user when the service provider was merely a conduit for the transmission (i.e., transmitting, routing, providing connections) (17 U.S.C. § 512(a) (2000)) or temporarily storing material that was generated by a person other than the service provider (17 U.S.C. § 512(b) (2000)). In either case, the service provider must not have modified or altered the material or selected the recipient of the transmission.

With respect to information residing on a system or network at the direction of a user, the service provider is not liable if it did not have actual or constructive notice that the material was infringing, did not receive a financial benefit directly attributable to the infringing activity, and it removed or disabled access to the material on notification of claimed infringement (17 U.S.C. § 512(c) (2000)). Under the same conditions, a service provider is not liable for referring or "linking" users to on-line locations containing infringing material through such information location tools as a directory, index, reference, or hyperlink (17 U.S.C. § 512(d) (2000)).

Service providers qualifying for liability limitations in subsections (a)–(d) are shielded from damage awards. Additionally, section 512(j) limits the availability of injunctive relief against eligible service providers. The limitations on liability apply only if the service provider has designated an agent to receive notifications of alleged infringements. Agent contact information must be available to the public through an accessible Web site and by providing the Copyright Office with the name, address, phone number, and electronic mail address of the agent. The Copyright Office has published interim regulations detailing this registration (37 C.F.R. pt. 201 (2000)).

Under section 512(i), notification of a claimed infringement must be in writing and provided to the agent of the service provider and must include the following: identification of the copyrighted work claimed to have been infringed, identification of the material claimed to be infringing, contact information for the complaining party, and a statement that the use was not authorized. In addition, the notice must be verified by a physical or electronic signature of the copyright owner or the agent of the owner. Even if the notice fails to comply with all these provisions, the service provider must take reasonable steps to contact the complaining party to obtain additional information if the service provider intends to avail itself of the liability limitations provided.

Furthermore, the service provider is eligible for these liability limitations under section 512(i) only if it adopts and reasonably implements a policy that provides for termination of a user's account under "appropriate circumstances" as defined by law. In addition, the service provider must accommodate and not interfere with technology designed to identify and protect copyrighted works.

Section 512(e) creates special protection for nonprofit educational service providers when a faculty member or graduate student employee infringes a copyright while performing certain teaching or research functions. The conditions attached to this exemption are that (1) the faculty member or graduate student employee's infringing activities do not involve providing on-line access to instructional materials or materials recommended for a course taught at the institution by the employee within the preceding three years; (2) within that three-year period, the institution received no more than two notifications of claimed infringement by the employee; and (3) the institution provides all users with information regarding compliance with copyright law. Presumably, compliance with this education requirement may be achieved by providing access to the institution's copyright policy or any other material that promotes compliance with federal copyright law. It is noteworthy that this provision only provides protection for the institution in the role of service provider; it does not limit the liability of the individual infringer (i.e., professor or graduate assistant).

Where the service provider is entitled to limited liability under section 512, the statute allows only limited injunctive remedies against a service provider. If infringement is determined, the court may grant injunctive relief restraining a service provider from providing access to a particular site or a particular user on the provider's system or network or other injunctive relief deemed necessary by the court to prevent the infringing activity, provided that such relief is the least burdensome to the service provider of any alternative remedies.

The DMCA also addressed technical aspects of copyright protection and management by adding Chapter 12 to the Copyright Act. That chapter prohibits the circumvention of technological protection for copyrighted works and tampering with copyright management information used to identify and protect copyright owners. This statute prohibits the manufacture, import, or trafficking in any technology or device (or even engaging in the industry supporting or assisting the development of such technology or device) that is designed to circumvent a protective technological measure for a copyrighted work and has limited use other than circumvention. Nonprofit libraries and educational institutions are permitted to access a commercial copyrighted work for the sole purpose of determining whether to acquire a copy of the work, provided, however, that no copy of the work is available in any other form (17 U.S.C. § 1201(d) (1998)) and that the institution does not use this access for commercial advantage or financial gain.

The service provider also may engage in permissible acts of security testing if the access is for the purpose of good faith testing, investigating, or correcting a security flaw. If the information derived from the security testing is used solely to promote or ensure the security of the system and is not used or maintained in a manner that facilitates infringement, there is no violation of the Act.

Remedies

Notwithstanding the liability limitations under the DMCA, other instances of copyright infringement can result in both civil remedies and criminal penalties. A copyright owner may seek a preliminary or permanent injunction where liability is established and there is a threat of continuing infringement (17 U.S.C. § 502 (1998)). The court may order impounding and, as part of the final judgment, destruction of the infringing copies (17 U.S.C. § 503 (1998)). A copyright owner may elect to recover actual damages (the amount of the owner's losses plus any profits of the infringer attributable to the act of infringement) (17 U.S.C. § 504(b) (1998)) or statutory damages that can range from $750 to $30,000 per work infringed. (These amounts were recently increased by the passage of the Digital Theft Deterrence and Copyright Damages Improvement Act of 1999, Pub. L. No. 106-160 (Dec. 9, 1999).) If the infringer can show that he or she was not aware and had no reason to believe that the activity constituted an infringement, the court may reduce the amount of statutory damages to a sum not less than $200. Should the copyright owner be able to show that the infringement was willful, the court may increase statutory damages up to $100,000 (17 U.S.C. § 504(c)(2) (1998)).

Under the Copyright Act, a judge may remit statutory damages (damages that may be imposed without proof of actual harm to the copyright owner) against a nonprofit educational institution, its employees, or its agents for copying they performed when they had reasonable grounds to believe that the copying was fair use of the material (17 U.S.C. § 504(c)(2) (1998)).

Despite the limitations on awards, it should be noted that Congress has specifically allowed copyright owners to collect damages from public colleges and universities by enacting the Copyright Remedy Clarification Act (CRCA) in 1990. Prior to that time, several federal appellate courts had held that the Eleventh Amendment prevented the damage provisions of the Copyright Act from being applied to state agencies, including public institutions of higher education (*see* Burgoyne, 1992). A recent case in the Fifth Circuit, however, has held that the CRCA was an improper abrogation of state sovereign immunity and that the Eleventh Amendment protects public higher education institutions against copyright claims in federal courts (*see* Chavez v. Art Publico Press, No. 93-2881, 200 U.S. App. LEXIS 2490 (Feb. 18, 2000)). Thus the sovereign immunity of state institutions for copyright and trademark violations is not resolved and continues to be the source of debate for the courts and legislature.

The copyright owner may recover attorney fees at the discretion of the court (17 U.S.C. § 505 (1998)). Criminal sanctions may be levied against infringers if the infringement was willful and for the purposes of commercial advantage or private financial gain. Additional civil remedies are imposed if there is circumvention of copyright protection (i.e., decryption, deactivation, bypass, or impairment of a technological protection measure that controls access to a work). In addition, criminal penalties are available for willful violations and for violations for commercial advantage; however, these do not apply to educational institutions.

Limitations/Fair Use

There are limits to the exclusive rights of copyright owners to reproduce, distribute, perform, display, and prepare derivatives of copyrighted works. Section 107 of the Copyright Act states in pertinent part that "the fair use of a copyrighted work . . ., for purposes such as criticism, comment, news reporting, teaching (including multiple copies for classroom use), scholarship or research, is not an infringement of copyright." Fair use is an affirmative defense to claims of copyright infringement and is determined on a case-by-case basis, with reference to the four factors set forth in Section 107:

1. The purpose and character of the use, including whether such use is of a commercial nature or is for nonprofit educational purposes

2. The nature of the copyrighted work

3. The amount and substantiality of the portion used in relation to the copyrighted work as a whole

4. The effect of the use on the potential market for or value of the copyrighted work

The United States Supreme Court has stated that all of the factors are to be explored and the results weighed together in light of the purposes of copyright. As for the first factor, the Supreme Court announced a presumption against fair use for commercial purposes (*see* Sony v. Universal City Studios, 464 U.S. 417 (1984)). When commercial use of copyrighted materials is involved, the burden is on a defendant to prove that a particular commercial use is fair.

Generally, the fair use standard will be satisfied if it is used for nonprofit educational purposes. Even in some educational contexts, however, reproduction of copyrighted materials has not been found to be fair use. For example, courts have denied fair use where a teacher reproduced another teacher's work in text materials (Marcus v. Rowbery, 695 F.2d 1171 (9th Cir. 1983)); where a school system taped educational broadcasts for later use in classrooms (Encyclopaedia Britannica Educ. Corp. v. Crooks, 558 F. Supp. 1247 (W.D.N.Y. 1983)); and where an off-campus copy shop copied and distributed photocopies of anthologies containing portions of textbooks and periodicals (Basic Books v. Kinko's Graphics, 758 F. Supp. 1522 (S.D.N.Y. 1991)).

The second and third factors set forth in the statute tend to have a less significant role in litigation to date but nevertheless warrant examination by the court. The nature of the copyrighted work generally weighs in favor of the copyright owner when unpublished works are copied, and in favor of the alleged infringer when published or factual works are copied. This factor may become more important in future decisions if the court determines that digitized works should be treated differently from works in conventional print form. The test for the third factor—amount and substantiality of the work—is easily met as the copying of a small portion of the work (if it is determined to be the "heart" of the work) will constitute infringement. For example, in *Harper & Row Publishers* v. *Nations Enterprises,* 471 U.S. 539, 569 (1985), the copying of a mere three hundred words was held to be infringing.

The most significant factor has been repeatedly identified as the economic effect of the use. Numerous Supreme Court decisions establish a presumption of market harm to the copyright owner in most cases where the use is commercial, unless it can be demonstrated that no existing or potential market exists or that the copyrighted work has been transformed (i.e., a parody). Some proponents of users' rights advocate that the harm to the economic interest should not be presumed but that courts should consider the date, price, and economic life of the copyrighted work, together with the accessibility of the work and the availability of copies, and that a plaintiff should be required to provide evidence of economic harm. Notwithstanding these arguments, the general rule continues to be that any use of a copyrighted work that has an adverse impact on the economic interests of the copyright owner will not constitute fair use of the work.

The fourth factor is not only the most critical to a determination of fair use but promises to be the most difficult to overcome in proving fair use in the Internet environment. One commentator observed that "the nature of the Internet itself militates heavily against a fair use finding. Unlike any other available reproduction and distribution technology, the Internet has the potential, with a few strokes of the keyboard, to enable a single infringer to instantly make copies of protected works available to millions of people, who may in turn copy and disseminate the work. As a result . . ., courts have been quick to find that the market effects of Internet infringement are severe" (Price, 1996).

Although the courts have not yet reviewed a case involving fair use of on-line material by an educational institution, some insight may be gleaned from the on-line infringement cases to date. In *Frena* and *MAPHIA*, the respective courts considered the fair use defense raised by the defendants. In considering the first element of fair use in those cases, the courts found that the purpose and character of the use was purely commercial. Furthermore, the nature of the works (photographs and video games) were highly original and the entire work was copied. Finally, both courts found that there was a substantial adverse impact on the potential market for, or value of, the copyrighted works that weighed against a finding of fair use.

Given the weight accorded to the fourth factor and the obvious power of the Internet for extensive copying and distribution, it appears that the fair use defense to copyright infringement may be in jeopardy in the electronic setting. Nevertheless, network users at an educational institution with no commercial intentions may make a case for continued fair use if it makes a strong showing on the first three factors.

Implied License

As discussed previously, a copyright owner may license others to use a copyrighted work; to the extent that the owner has authorized or licensed others to use the copyrighted material, the owner is prevented from asserting exclusive control. In many cases these licenses are explicit, such as a shrinkwrap license on computer software packages. According to contract law principles, a license may also be implied in certain circumstances. For example, a copyright owner who posts his or her copyrighted material on the Internet knows that others will access that material, reproducing it on their own computer screen. Although the copyright owner has not expressly stated so, there is an implied license for other Internet users to view the original image, provided that the copyright owner authorized the placing of the material on a Web site. The implied license extends only to the personal use of the user accessing it; there is no license to distribute the materials to others or to use it for financial benefit. Although the extent of this implied license is a matter of some debate, it is important to note that the posting of copyrighted material on the Internet does not place the material in the public domain unless the copyright owner explicitly so states. Furthermore, if the person posting the material does not have the right to post the item in the first place, then no implied license can take place.

Net Act

Another piece of federal legislation that impacts computer network users is the No Electronic Theft (NET) Act (the NET Act) (Pub. L. No. 105-147 (1997)) that provides greater protection for copyright owners by attaching criminal liability and penalties for infringers who reproduce or distribute by electronic means one or more copies of copyrighted works valued at more than $1,000. The statute was a legislative response to the judicial decision in *United States v. LaMacchia*, 871 F. Supp. 535 (D. Mass. 1994), a case in which a student at the Massachusetts Institute of Technology was charged with violating a federal wire fraud statute. The facts alleged that defendant LaMacchia encouraged owners of computer games to upload copyrighted games to a bulletin board server (BBS), whereupon the defendant would transfer the games to another BBS for downloading by other users. No compensation was paid to the copyright holders of the computer games nor did LaMacchia benefit financially from these activities. The federal district court dismissed the claims against LaMacchia on the basis that copyrights were not protected under the federal wire fraud statute. The court also found that the sanctions for criminal infringement of copyright did not apply where there was no financial gain by the infringer. In dicta, the court noted that Congress needed to change the law if it wanted to criminalize such activity (*id.* at 545).

The NET Act discourages similar activity in the future by including in the definition of financial gain the "receipt or expectation of receipt of anything of value, including the receipt of other copyrighted works." The statute enables prosecution of a person who steals or helps others steal copyrighted works regardless of personal profit. In addition, the NET Act also clarifies the threshold for claims of criminal copyright infringement. Whereas copyright law previously provided that criminal penalties could be imposed for anyone who infringes copyright willfully and for purposes of commercial advantage and private financial gain, the new language imposes criminal penalties where a person reproduces or distributes, including by electronic means, during any 180-day period, one or more copies of copyrighted works that have a total retail value of more than $1,000 (17 U.S.C. § 506(a), as amended).

Implications for Higher Education

Following this review of the rights afforded to copyright owners and the manner in which infringement may occur during the use of Internet services, it is readily apparent that there is substantial activity by students, faculty, and staff on most university campuses that could open the door for potential liability. For example, students regularly download digitized photographs from newsgroups to which they subscribe via university-provided Internet accounts. Downloading these photographs to the student's personal computer involves making a copy; if the student then chooses to copy the work to a disk or to print it out, additional copies are generated that may constitute a violation of the copyright owner's exclusive right to reproduce the copyrighted work (provided the original copy the student downloaded was not authorized by the copyright owner). Likewise, a professor who uploads a copyrighted work to a newsgroup or listserv for his students is both reproducing and distributing the work. As noted earlier, public display rights may be implicated simply by viewing copyrighted photos on the computer screen, a fairly common practice by students, especially at universities that have more sophisticated communications software that interfaces with the Web.

Unquestionably, direct infringement of copyright can (and probably does) occur on a regular basis. Under certain circumstances, the individual engaging in such an infringement may be liable under the Copyright Act, or even subject to criminal sanctions under the Net Act. Individuals can avoid liability by establishing that a work on the Internet has been authorized by the copyright owner or is in the public domain and by obtaining permission from the copyright owner for use outside the scope of fair use or the implied license. Users can assert the defense of fair use if the copyrighted material is being used for the purpose of criticism, comment, news reporting, teaching, scholarship, or research. Fair use, once established, is a complete defense to infringement. For institutions of higher education, the fair use doctrine is particularly important because there can be no determination of contributory or vicarious liability if the primary activity is not infringing.

Although the courts have not yet been presented with the fair use defense raised by an educational institution in the Internet context, it is reasonable to expect that courts will approach claims of fair use in that context just as they would in traditional environments. In that regard, a court will consider the four factors set forth in the statute. Using an earlier example, one might assume that a professor's posting of copyrighted works to a class listserv would be justified as fair use as it would be used for teaching purposes. If fair use is established, neither the professor nor the institution would be liable for copyright infringement; unfortunately, there are no guarantees that the time and expense of litigation could be avoided altogether, since fair use determinations are made on a case-by-case basis. The most conservative approach is to seek permission from the copyright owner.

Institutional Liability

Assuming that direct infringement has taken place by a user on the campus network, the question then becomes to what extent will the university be held liable for the acts of its students, faculty, and staff in its role as the provider of the computer network. The DMCA specifically limits institutional liability for on-line infringement by campus network users, provided the referencing work is not university content (i.e., has been placed on the network by the university) and provided that the institution meets the specific requirements for exemption set forth in the statute. Failure to meet the requirements means that the institution may be forced to litigate a case of alleged copyright infringement. Even when the copyright owner can obtain injunctive relief only under the DMCA (17 U.S.C. § 512(j) (2000)), the college or university still faces a court appearance that might otherwise be avoided. Furthermore, if it is established that the work is not one that is covered by the Act, (i.e., the educational provider received a direct financial benefit from the infringing activity) the copyright owner would be entitled to seek monetary damages from the college or university.

It is clear that the institution cannot escape all responsibility for infringing activities occurring on its network; it must expeditiously remove or disable access on receipt of written notice from the copyright owner. If the institution removes or blocks material that turns out to be noninfringing, it is also insulated from liability for privacy and free speech violations alleged by network users.

Given the legal framework, what approach should the institution take to students storing MP3s on its server or distributing MP3s from the campus network system? Because an institution may not engage in content monitoring of its network, it may not be aware of specific instances of MP3 storage on the network. However, if the institution receives written notification of an alleged copyright violation from the owner, the institution must investigate and take steps to remove the infringing material from the network. Some institutions have addressed the MP3 issue by blocking access to the MP3 trading application "Napster," basing its elimination on the volume of traffic it creates for the institutional network.

As for graduate students who download graphics for use in their dissertation without permission, they may be directly liable to the copyright owner unless they can establish the defense of fair use. The institution, however, will be shielded from liability for any monetary damages in this instance if the eligibility requirements of the DMCA are met. The faculty member who posts copyrighted material without permission may be spared from direct liability only if fair use is established. If no fair use exists, the institution is not entitled to special protection afforded by the DMCA because the copyrighted materials were for a course taught at the institution by the faculty member. Thus, where an employee of the institution is violating copyright in his or her teaching role, the institution may be held liable if direct infringement is proved.

Trademark Infringement

In addition to concerns over copyright violations, network users and providers must be aware that trademark infringement and unfair competition claims may arise from Internet use by students or faculty when the material downloaded or downloaded and distributed involves a commercial entity. Claims of copyright and trademark infringement often will be brought in an intellectual property case, although the rights arise under independent federal laws.

A *trademark* is any word, name, symbol, or device, or any combination of these, that serves to identify or distinguish one organization's goods or services from those of another organization. A *service mark* is the same as a trademark except that it identifies services rather than goods. The purpose of a trademark is to identify the source of products or services and to distinguish the trademark owner's goods or services from those of another. In the United States, trademark ownership rights arise through continued use of a mark. The owner of the trademark is entitled to exclusive use of the mark and can prevent other parties from using a similar mark that would create confusion for the public. The Lanham Act (15 U.S.C. §§ 1051 et seq. (1998)) serves as the foundation for federal trademark law and is based on the Commerce Clause of the United States Constitution. To register a trademark under federal law, the owner of the mark must demonstrate that the mark is used in commerce regulated by Congress (i.e., interstate commerce or foreign commerce).

In order to establish a case for trademark infringement, the plaintiff need only demonstrate that the mark is owned or associated with the plaintiff and that the defendant's use of an allegedly infringing mark is likely to cause confusion or mistake among the public. The plaintiff does not have to prove that any person was actually confused or mistaken by the defendant's use; all that is required is the "likelihood" of confusion, mistake, or deception. In addition, a showing of intent is unnecessary to establish a violation of trademark law. Nevertheless, if the acts have been committed with knowledge and intent that the imitation would cause confusion or mistake, then the owner may be entitled to profits or damages (15 U.S.C. § 1114(1)(b) (1998)). A trademark owner may also claim unfair competition against any person who uses a trademark in such a way as to cause confusion or to deceive consumers about its relationship with the trademark owner (15 U.S.C. § 1125(a)(1)(A)(1998)).

Existing legal precedent applies the available remedies for trademark infringement and unfair competition occurring through the unauthorized use of trademarks electronically. In *Playboy Enterprises* v. *Frena* and *Sega Enterprises Ltd.* v. *MAPHIA*, cited earlier, the plaintiffs also claimed trademark infringement and unfair competition because the downloaded photographs (*Frena*) and video games (*MAPHIA*) carried the trademark names of the respective plaintiffs. In the first case, the court found that the mere appearance of the Playboy trademark on the downloaded photographs falsely suggested an affiliation with the trademark owner that was likely to cause confusion on the part of those who saw the photographs and therefore constituted trademark infringement. Similarly, the *MAPHIA* court found that a game copied from the defendant's bulletin board that began with a screen showing the federally registered SEGA trademark would inevitably cause confusion on the part of third parties who might see the copied games. Accordingly, the respective plaintiffs were entitled to damages for trademark infringement. In general then, downloading and distributing images that bear a trademark may constitute infringement under certain circumstances.

Domain Names

The use of Internet domain names has also been challenged as a source of trademark infringement. A domain name is a technique for identification on the Internet that is made possible by a system that utilizes a Domain Name Service (DNS) database to link numerical computer addresses (part of the Internet Protocol) with mnemonic alphanumeric equivalents called Internet domain names (Dueker, 1996). The problem arises because the technical constraints (i.e., maximum of twenty-four letters per name, no capitalization) of Internet domain naming preclude organizations from distinguishing themselves through stylized formats that might be used in other contexts. Entities with similar names may find it difficult to keep their domain names unique enough to avoid confusion and, even worse, inadvertent infringement.

To complicate the name confusion, domain name registers generally register domain names on a first-come, first-served basis. Anyone can register a name for approximately $100, provided the name has not already been registered. Moreover, no central directory exists to assist a user in finding the correct domain name. As a result, a user may enter the name of an organization or institution and connect to a site that has a similar domain name to the one sought. In the case of a business attempting to facilitate communication with a customer base, the results can be detrimental, especially if potential customers are directed to the Web site of a competing business (*see, e.g.,* Zippo Manufacturing Co. v. Zippo Dot Com, Inc., 952 F. Supp. 1119 (W.D. Pa. 1997); *see also,* MTV Networks v. Curry, 867 F. Supp. 202 (S.D.N.Y. 1994)).

Trademark infringement cases involving domain names have not been limited to commercial enterprises. In the case of *Columbia University v. Columbia/HCA Healthcare Corp.* (964 F. Supp. 733 (S.D.N.Y. 1997)), a New York district court considered a dispute over the right to use the mark Columbia by itself or in combination with other words. The plaintiff used the name and owned the federal registration for the service mark Columbia University in connection with educational services. Moreover, the plaintiff maintained an Internet Web page at Columbia.edu through which a user could link to a medical information service. The plaintiff was affiliated with Columbia-Presbyterian Medical Center, which also linked its Web site to the plaintiff's. The defendant was one of the largest providers of health care services in the United States, operating approximately 340 hospitals, 130 surgery centers, and over 200 home health care agencies, all of which use the Columbia name in some form. Beginning in May 1995, the defendant put up its home page on the Internet at Columbia.net. The home page appeared under a banner bearing the word Columbia along with the defendant's design and logo style for the Columbia name. Using hypertext, the Web page was linked to Columbia Physician's Corner, which provided transcripts of real-time on-line conversations with Columbia physicians on a variety of medical topics of interest to the public. There was a linked Web page for a computer bulletin board where physicians could post or view articles about their area of specialty. The defendant had also contracted with America Online to provide medical information and referral services for America Online subscribers and other Internet users under the Internet domain name Columbia.net.

In 1996, Columbia University filed a lawsuit claiming trademark infringement and unfair competition. The court eventually dismissed the plaintiff's claims on both legal and equitable grounds, determining that the plaintiff's exclusive use of its trademark was limited to educational services, not to medical or health care services. Furthermore, defendant Columbia/HCA Healthcare could not claim dilution of its trademark when the evidence indicated that there were over one hundred federal trademarks that incorporated the Columbia name. The court found that the services rendered by the parties to the case were distinguishable: the plaintiff provided educational services, among which was medical training; conversely, the defendant was a licensed provider of health care and medical services. Therefore, the plaintiff could not establish consumer confusion that would result in injury to Columbia University.

Higher education may seem an unlikely arena for trademark infringement activity, but the growing number of university Web sites could be problematic, especially if creative students take advantage of technological capabilities without being aware of the consequences of their actions (i.e., linking to a commercial Web site in a way that implies authority to use trademarks or even engaging in commercial enterprises from one's residence hall).

The university also needs to protect its own trademarks from infringement by third parties hoping to benefit from use of the institution's good name. In fact, speculators have attempted to capitalize on the names of several universities by registering the name of the institution followed by .com instead of .edu in an attempt to promote a private business. Some universities have begun to take a proactive approach to protect their trademarked names by registering their own name followed by .com (see Thompson).

In addition to early registration of domain names, colleges and universities may also have administrative recourse. Network Solutions, Inc. (NSI), under contract with the National Science Foundation, instituted a Domain Name Dispute Policy in 1998 (<www.internic.net>). Under that policy the institution can send NSI proof of ownership and written notice to the domain name registrant describing the infringement, provided that the offending domain name was created after a university trademark was registered. If the domain name owner cannot produce proof of ownership of the mark satisfactory to NSI, NSI will place a hold on the use of the name. Should the domain name registrant file a lawsuit, however, the institution will be forced to engage in litigation in the forum chosen by the domain name holder (*see* Zebrak, 1999).

Another Internet phenomenon that has arisen from the lack of regulation of domain name registration is the practice of *cybersquatting*. Cybersquatting involves the registration of well-known trademarks by non-trademark-holders who then try to sell back the names to the trademark owner. In late 1999, Congress passed the Anti-Cybersquatting Consumer Protection Act (ACPA) to prevent this type of activity. The new Act makes a person civilly liable to the trademark owner for abusive and bad-faith registration of distinctive marks as Internet domain names with the intent to profit from the mark. In order to prevail on a claim under the ACPA, the plaintiff must demonstrate that the defendant acted with a bad-faith intent to profit from the mark (15 U.S.C. § 1125(d)(1)(A)(i)). The statute lists nine factors to assist courts in determining whether the defendant acted with bad-faith intent (15 U.S.C. § 1125(d)(1)(B)(I)); *see also* Sporty's Farm v. Sportsman Market, Inc., 202 F.3d 489 (2d Cir. 2000)). Unlike traditional trademark law, however, the potential for liability under the ACPA exists without regard to the goods or services of the parties involved in the lawsuit. Consequently, a child with the nickname "Pokey" could be liable under the ACPA to a corporate toymaker of Pokey toys. (For additional analysis of the ACPA, *see* Grossman & Hift, 2000.)

Given the development of dispute resolution policies for domain name controversies and the statutory remedy created by the ACPA, higher education institutions appear to have adequate recourse in the event that their domain name is used by unrelated third parties. Plans to introduce new domain suffixes (e.g., .shop, .banc, .firm) in November, 2000 are likely to create new controversies for universities who want to protect institutional trademarks (Foster, 2000).

Web-Linking

A practice unique to the World Wide Web information network has resulted in claims of copyright and trademark infringement. *Web-linking* is the process of linking one Web page to another page in its own site or to a page on a different Web site through the use of HyperText Markup Language or HTML.

The problem arises when links are made to Web pages that confuse the person following the link about the source of information on the linked-to page. Although no court has yet ruled on it, the practice of Web-linking may constitute a violation of copyright law when the linking occurs against the express wishes of the copyright owner. In other words, the implied license that the copyright owner gives to the user accessing the material may be modified by explicit conditions set forth on the owner's Web sites. If that owner specifically prohibits linking to its Web site, then doing so may result in contributory copyright infringement, particularly where the establishment of the link encourages others to infringe a copyright.

Another troublesome practice associated with Web-linking is made possible by the use of *framing*, which allows the linking site to show only a portion of the target site's page surrounded or framed by the material prepared by the linking site, thus altering the appearance of the page created by the target site. This intrusive practice was the subject of litigation in *Washington Post Co. v. Total News, Inc.*, No. 97 Civ. 1190 (PKL) (S.D.N.Y. 1997), in which the plaintiff alleged trademark infringement and copyright violations against the operator of a Web site known as totalnews.com. A visitor to that site who clicked on a hyperlink to one of the plaintiff's publications would not see the entirety of the plaintiff's site; rather, the visitor would see only a portion of the page without its identifying information, including its uniform resource locator (URL). Masking that part of the plaintiff's page was the defendant's logo,

URL, and advertisements, making it appear as though the information belonged to the defendant. In its complaint, the plaintiff alleged that this practice of obscuring the plaintiff's identifying information constituted misappropriation, trademark dilution under the Lanham Act, and copyright infringement as well as multiple claims under New York State law. In a settlement agreement that disposed of the lawsuit, the defendants agreed to link to the plaintiff's Web site via hyperlinks that consisted of the names of linked sites in plain text and not to use any Web site in a manner likely to imply affiliation or endorsement by the Washington Post or to cause confusion, mistake, or deception to the public.

Some states have attempted to deal with unauthorized Web-linking through legislation. For example, Georgia enacted an Internet Fraud Statute (Ga. Code Ann. § 16-9-93.1(a) (1996)) that imposed criminal sanctions for transmitting data that falsely implied permission or authorization to use another entity's trade name, registered trademark, logo, legal or official seal, or copyrighted symbol when such permission or authorization had not been obtained. This statute was subsequently held unconstitutional on the basis that it was overbroad, leaving the practice of Web-linking unregulated.

Links and frames present problems that are unique to the Internet. Although no legal precedent exists yet to guide these practices, common sense dictates that if one directly links to content that is normally framed elsewhere, the owners are likely to object. Where a linking page surrounds another's material with its own ads or makes it appear that the linking site is the source of the material, the courts may find a violation of copyright or trademark law. (For additional discussion of this topic, see Field, 2000 and Templeton, 2000.)

Internal Ownership Considerations

Thus far this chapter has dealt solely with the potential for liability when a claim or lawsuit is brought by a third party against a university. The importance of these considerations notwithstanding, the university community also has intellectual property that it must protect from infringement. A precursor to enforcing the legal protections available to the university under the 1976 Copyright Act is a determination of ownership of a copyright. The electronic venue has created some new issues with which the institution must grapple.

For institutions that are engaging in distance education by offering and delivering courses via the Web, the commitment on the part of the university in providing the resources and on the part of the faculty member in preparing materials to upload is far greater than in the traditional classroom. Putting course materials into digitized form does not just involve scanning lecture notes; it often necessitates using multimedia and creative methods of delivering tests and other coursework. These methods are outside the scope of traditional teaching and can raise new questions regarding ownership of course materials that had not been problematic in the past.

For example, suppose a professor works for over a year developing materials to be used in a Web-based course being offered through the university as a part of its regular curriculum. In order to have time to put the materials together, the faculty member is given release time from his regular course load. In addition, he extensively uses the equipment owned by the university and the service of technicians hired by the university to create multimedia presentations. At the conclusion of the distance learning course, the professor decides to take a position at another university. He believes that the course materials he has developed belong to him, may be revised at his discretion, and may be used in subsequent courses at his new institution. Because of the substantial use of university-owned resources, however, the university wants to retain ownership of the materials to be used in future offerings. In the absence of definitive policies or a prior agreement, the dispute can ultimately result in litigation.

Traditionally, at many universities materials authored by professors in the course of their professional duties of teaching and research were considered to be owned by the professor. There is early case law preceding the 1976 Act that made university professors an exception to the work-for-hire doctrine set forth in the 1909 Copyright Act (*see* Williams v. Weisser, 78 Cal. Rptr. 542 (Super. Ct. App. 1969); Sherrell v. Grieves, 57 Wash. L. Rep (Sup. Ct. D.C. 1920)). Most legal scholars and subsequent court decisions have concluded that the 1976 Act terminated the exception for faculty work (*see* DuBoff, 1985 and Simon, 1982). Although some courts have suggested that the academic exception to the work-for-hire doctrine may still exist, the majority view is that the copyright ownership of faculty works vests with the institution if created within the scope of employment (*see, e.g.,* Weinstein v. University of Illinois, 811 F.2d 1091 (7th Cir. 1987)).

Although there appears to be no statutory exception for faculty work, many university copyright policies state that the copyright of certain faculty works belong to the professor. These policies contractually bind the university and satisfy the transfer of ownership interest requirements under the Act. As a result, absent special circumstances or agreements to the contrary, faculty have been comfortable in the assurance that they would retain copyright ownership of their intellectual property, a presumption that is borne out by the scarcity of litigation in this area.

In the past the expenses incurred by the university in the research and creation of written work by the faculty was customarily limited to providing office space, secretarial help, and library services. With the advent of distance education, the cost associated with the production of a multimedia presentation is much greater, not only in terms of the technology infrastructure required, but for supplemental pay for faculty, curriculum specialists, and technology support personnel. The end product—digitized electronic course materials—may be valuable, with other educators, institutions, or private industry interested in acquiring them.

Ostensibly, the competing interests for the university are to benefit financially while promoting an environment in which the faculty is encouraged to be creative and pursue intellectual breakthroughs without being exploited by the economic concerns of the institution. Determination of proprietary interests in electronic course materials is a central issue for both administrators and faculty. Given the potential conflict that may arise between university interests and individual faculty creator interests, it is critical to make a determination of ownership early in the process of course development.

In 1998, the Campus Computing Survey revealed that most campuses had not developed policies to address intellectual property ownership issues; only one-third of research universities report some type of policy governing faculty-developed intellectual property, one-fourth of public four-year colleges and community colleges, and less than one-sixth of four-year private colleges. Author Kenneth Green observed that great expectations for on-line instruction as a cash machine led to "tense discussions between faculty and administrators about institutional copyright policies affecting a wide range of materials and resources that faculty routinely develop as part of their scholarly and instructional activities" (*The Campus Computing Project*, <ericir.syr.edu/Projects/Campus_computing/1998>).

Ownership Models

For institutions that have or are developing copyright ownership policies, several different ownership models are being followed. The first model assumes ownership of the work by the faculty member. The faculty may assign ownership to the institution, thereby relinquishing management and control of the work (and standing to sue for copyright infringement) in exchange for some form of remuneration. The faculty author may also retain ownership but grant the university a nonexclusive license; that is, the right to use the materials when the course is taught by someone other than the faculty author. The author and university may also agree to share profits from commercialization, depending on the university's contribution to the work.

The second model assumes ownership by the university or college under the work-for-hire doctrine. The university retains control for distribution and licensing, and the ability to pursue copyright infringers. The faculty author would be entitled to either royalties for subsequent use of the work and a nonexclusive license or a nonexclusive license or royalties to use the materials in classes taught elsewhere.

A third model assumes that the faculty creating distance learning materials is an independent contractor, and the creation of the work would be outside the scope of employment and therefore the faculty author would have ownership and the ability to assign or license the work as in the first model. (For further discussion of these models, *see* Burk, 1997.)

The first task of the institution is to decide what approach or model will be implemented; thereafter it is advisable that the agreement regarding ownership between the individual faculty member and the institution be reduced to writing in clear, unambiguous terms. This should be accomplished prior to the creation of the work to avoid confusion once the "expression of ideas" has taken place and copyright ownership is determined by law.

Once ownership has been established, copyright law dictates the ability of the owner to pursue third parties for copyright infringement of distance learning materials or any other copyrighted work owned by the university. As in the traditional environment, the full benefits of copyright cannot be achieved without registration of the work, and tracking the registrations may be a time-consuming and expensive task for the institution. Licensing of these works may be equally as costly. Many larger universities have technology transfer offices or some type of intellectual property management programs in place, whereas smaller colleges may not have the resources to manage a large copyright portfolio. For digitized works, vigorous protection of university intellectual property may require monitoring of the Internet for unauthorized copying.

Recommendations

College and university administrators can aid network system users and protect the institution from unnecessary litigation by educating them about the legal ramifications of copying digitized materials. This can best be accomplished by dissemination of a policy that is written in understandable terms to the broad spectrum of individuals that comprise the university community. The following suggestions may facilitate the formation of campus policies and address the legal concerns raised in this chapter.

1. **Compliance with DMCA requirements.** In order to take advantage of the limited liability that the DMCA provides, the institution must

    • Designate an agent to receive notifications of claimed infringements, make the contact information for that agent available through its service (i.e., on its Web site), and provide the United States Copyright Office with the name and address of the agent

    • Adopt, reasonably implement, and inform its users of a policy that provides for termination of a user's account in cases of repeated infringement

    • Include language in the computer use policy that the institution has an unequivocal right to terminate access in instances where users have engaged in copyright infringement on more than one occasion

    • Disseminate, either on-line or by hard copy, the rules regarding copyright infringement to students, faculty, and staff

    • Advise users that they do not share the university's liability limitations for their direct infringement of

another's copyrighted work, irrespective of the ease
with which it can be accessed on-line, and of the
potential criminal and civil consequences of
infringement

2. **Implement fair use guidelines.** Any information disseminated about copyright law would normally include a discussion of the fair use doctrine. Because the analysis of fair use is
difficult for most legislators, judges, and lawyers, it is likely
that the assessment will prove equally elusive to members of
the university community. To facilitate an understanding of
the fair use concept, the institution may choose to provide its
users with some guidelines covering the concept's application
in the educational setting.

An institution may formulate its own rules for assessing fair
use. At least one institution has set up a step-by-step process
that users can employ in their own fair use analysis (*see*
<www.utsystem.edu/ogc/intellectualproperty/copypol2.htm>
(visited April 1, 1999)). If this approach is undertaken, careful
attention must be paid to the four factors utilized in a legal
determination as educational purpose alone is not sufficient to
justify fair use. Other institutions have chosen to direct users to
websites that provide explanations of the fair use concept (e.g.,
<fairuse.stanford.edu>).

In general, guidelines should discourage downloading of all
or large parts of a copyrighted work; where copying is done, it
should be limited to the number of copies necessary and should
always contain attribution information. The most important
assessment is whether the use, even though for educational purposes, deprives the copyright owner of financial benefits that
would be realized but for the unauthorized copying.

3. **Provide copyright resources.** If budgetary constraints permit, provide a copyright resource office that can answer

questions and assist in obtaining copyright permission where fair use is contraindicated or questionable. Obtaining copyright permission is not necessarily costly or time-consuming; sometimes it can be achieved through one e-mail exchange with the copyright owner. Where funds or personnel are not available, or where the need is not sufficient to warrant a full-time operation, users should minimally be permitted to direct questions to university legal counsel. The creation of such a system will enhance the university community's understanding of intellectual property laws while reducing the likelihood of unauthorized use.

4. **Require permission for trademark use and linking.** The policy should clearly state that users do not have permission to use institutional trademarks or logos on their personal Web pages without first obtaining authorization to do so. Preventing users from such activity has a twofold purpose: first, it protects the interest that the institution has in its intellectual property; second, it prohibits individual users from holding themselves out as representatives of the university. Requiring authorization reduces the likelihood that liability will be imputed to the institution if a user is deemed to be acting on behalf of, or as an agent of, the institution. In instances where permission is given for use of university trademarks or logos, the institution can distance itself from an agency relationship by requiring the user to add a disclaimer (i.e., stating that the document does not represent the views of the institution) on posted information. With respect to linking, the university may want to expressly prohibit such a practice, particularly if the linking will burden the university server.

5. **Determine ownership of on-line course materials.** Determining ownership of digitized intellectual property is a prerequisite to enforcement of the exclusive rights of the

copyright holder; consequently, institutions must revisit their existing copyright policies (and possibly collective bargaining agreements) to ascertain whether the customary notions of ownership are applicable to on-line course materials and multimedia. If, for example, faculty have traditionally owned all course materials under an existing policy, any variation in ownership would require a change to the policy or a written contract between the faculty member and the institution that specifies the new ownership arrangement. Conversely, if the institution normally retains ownership of the course materials under the work-for-hire doctrine, a written contract assigning ownership to the faculty member would be requested to change ownership.

If the institution yields copyright ownership to an individual faculty member, the institution is no longer in a position to protect the property from infringement; only the faculty member can assert the exclusive rights of ownership. In that event, the institution should be released from any obligation to protect the faculty's copyright; in fact, contract language should be incorporated to have the faculty member hold the institution harmless in the event of infringement by a third party. This can be accomplished in the context of a separate written agreement for the development of the on-line course materials.

6. **Protect institutional copyrights.** If the institution holds copyright ownership in intellectual property developed by its faculty members, the institution may want to have certain encryption measures in place to prevent unauthorized copying. The institution also assumes responsibility for monitoring the Internet for potential infringement and for notifying other service providers if infringement is discovered. Ultimately, the institution bears the burden of instituting litigation and pursuing its remedies against infringers.

Conclusion

The legal issues surrounding intellectual property have always been a murky area, with legislators and courts attempting to balance the interests of authors and information consumers. The concerns surrounding their respective rights in an electronic forum have further muddied intellectual property waters, often resulting in strident calls for reconfiguration of existing laws to adapt to the new technology. In this turbulent environment, colleges and universities are expected to carry out a dual function: providing access to information for students, faculty, and staff, and protecting the intellectual property of the university from potential infringers. Notwithstanding the conflict inherent in those roles, it is important that users and administrators of campus networks be cognizant of current laws governing the use of digitized intellectual property.

2

Free Speech in Cyberspace

College and university campuses traditionally have been havens for free speech. Because of the historical role of higher education as "a marketplace of ideas," courts have taken a benevolent attitude toward free speech on college campuses, particularly if it is limited to the confines of the institution. The growing presence of computer networks provided by colleges and universities has added a new dimension to speech on campuses; institutions must be concerned not only about expression taking place within its physical environs but that taking place in cyberspace as well.

Compounding free speech issues is a developing Internet culture that is rigorously opposed to any form of regulation. An early example of this "don't tread on me" ethos occurred at Cornell University when a group calling itself On-line Freedom Fighters Anarchist Liberation sent satirical e-mail messages to more than twenty thousand students, staff, and faculty to protest Cornell's punishment of four students who were responsible for creating and sending misogynist e-mail. The overload temporarily disrupted the operation of the Cornell network (*see* Pavela, 1996).

This unforeseen consequence of the regulation of campus computer networks was made possible by the technology itself. Moreover, the backlash to disciplinary measures does not have to emanate from the university community; in the electronic environment, the whole world may be watching. In a genre of heightened awareness about free expression, individuals within the university community may receive support—financial and otherwise—to pursue purported violations of free speech as a result of overzealous or inappropriate regulation of campus computer networks. Groups such as the Electronic Frontier Foundation, the Center for Democratic Technology, and the ACLU have all been active and vocal proponents of on-line freedom. Some maintain legal staffs to assist in remedying alleged wrongs.

At the same time, however, university and college administrators are also charged with protecting the rights of others in the university community by maintaining an atmosphere in which insulting, obscene, or harassing speech is prohibited. The failure to do so can result in potential legal liability as well as negative publicity for the institution. Although these are not new issues, they are exacerbated when the behavior occurs on-line via the campus network. The university, as the provider of the campus system, must confront this new role and plan accordingly.

Network administrators are continually confronted with problems that have legal overtones. For example, does the institutional provider have to be concerned when its students make critical (potentially defamatory) remarks that travel over the campus network? Is the institution obliged to provide access to all sites available on the Internet? Administrators may also be faced with specific allegations of abuses occurring on-line. Suppose a female student claims that she is receiving obscene e-mails from other students. What is the appropriate institutional response and does that response change if the e-mails occur in the context of an on-line course?

As statutory and case law emerge, institutions must consider: the extent to which regulation is permitted or even advisable; when and how a campus system should be monitored; and the importance of carefully crafted policies as a preventive measure. To that end, this chapter examines the legal parameters in which expression can be restricted. It then reviews judicial decisions in Internet litigation and discusses their implications for higher education.

Much of the discussion centers on laws and constitutional provisions that affect public institutions because of the status of these institutions as subdivisions of the state, or state actors. Private institutions are not within the purview of some of these laws, but may be bound to follow mandates affecting public institutions if similar requirements are incorporated in their contracts, catalogs, faculty manuals, and institutional policies.

Legal Analysis of First Amendment Claims

The courts have been steadfast in reviewing free speech claims according to a strict scrutiny standard, permitting restriction only when a public institution is able to meet a two-pronged test by (1) proving a compelling government interest and (2) demonstrating that the restrictive practice is narrowly tailored in its application. If the institution fails to meet either prong of the test, the regulation will fail.

In analyzing a case alleging a free speech violation, the court will first determine if the restricted conduct constitutes expression and if the government limited or restricted the expression. For example, courts have held that distributing leaflets and collecting petitions on campus constitute expression; however, erecting a tent on school property does not (*see* State v. Ybarra, 550 P.2d 763 (Or. Ct. App. 1976)). If the expression does not fall within one of the categories of prohibited speech discussed in the sections that follow, then the court will look at the setting or forum in which the expression took place. For example, speech that takes place in an area traditionally (or by official policy) available to students or the entire university community for expressive activities will receive far more protection than those not undertaken in a public forum. However, if the expression involves a substantial disruption or invades the rights of others, it will not be protected under the First Amendment (Tinker v. Des Moines Sch. Dist., 393 U.S. 503 (1969)). The courts have repeatedly acknowledged that a public institution may regulate speech that is disruptive; however, such regulation must be based on something more substantial than mere suspicion or fear of possible disruption (Shamloo v. Mississippi State Bd. of Trustees, 620 F.2d 516 (5th Cir. 1980)).

Administrators have a greater ability to regulate expression that takes place as a part of school-sponsored activities. If the expression takes place in a forum designated as a nonpublic or closed forum (i.e., one that is not by tradition or use a forum for public communication), restrictions on the content of expression are permissible, provided that regulation is reasonable and does not discriminate based solely on the speaker's viewpoint.

Time, Place, and Manner Constraints

In addition to adopting regulations that prohibit disruption, public institutions may also promulgate reasonable regulations governing the time, place, and manner in which students conduct their speech-related activities (Healey v. James, 408 U.S. 169 (1972)). Time, place, and manner restrictions may only limit expression that is basically incompatible with the normal activity of a particular place at a particular time (Grayned v. Rockford, 408 U.S. 104, 116 (1972)). In general, these regulations will be upheld if they conform to a three-part judicial test that determines (1) they are justified without reference to the content of the regulated speech, (2) they are narrowly tailored to serve a significant government interest, and (3) they leave open ample channels for communication of the information (Clark v. Community for Creative Non-Violence, 468 U.S. 288 (1964)).

Given the requirement for narrow tailoring, university administrators must exercise caution when drafting or implementing any policies that purport to regulate the time, place, or manner in which speech takes place. In addition to the judicial parameters outlined above, these policies or regulations must not be too broad in scope. The overbreadth doctrine prohibits sweeping protected speech within the coverage of regulations designed to limit prohibited expression. In short, a university policy may be challenged as overbroad if it is worded so that it can be used to penalize students or faculty for having exercised their constitutionally protected right to expression.

Under the Fourteenth Amendment, a law, regulation, or policy may also be challenged as vague if it is so unclear that the person being regulated does not understand what is required or prohibited and can act accordingly. Vagueness principles are particularly important in speech-related activity on the theory that statutory vagueness could have a chilling effect on speech. In *Doe v. University of Michigan*, 721 F. Supp. 852 (E.D. Mich. 1989), a graduate student challenged the university's hate speech policy prohibiting any verbal or physical behavior that had the effect of stigmatizing or victimizing an individual on the basis of a number of different factors, including, but not limited to, race, sex, sexual orientation, age, marital status, or prior military status. The behavior was prohibited if it interfered with or created a hostile environment for the individual in pursuing academic or extracurricular activity.

The court held that the policy was unconstitutionally broad on its face because the wording sought to punish substantial amounts of protected speech. Furthermore, the use of the words *stigmatize, victimize,* and *interfere with* were vague; students would be unable to discern what speech was protected and what was prohibited. As a result of *Doe* and subsequent cases with similar results (*see, e.g.,* UVM Post v. Board of Regents of the Univ. of Wis. Sys., 774 F. Supp. 1163 (E.D. Wis. 1991); Iota Xi Chap. of Sigma Chi Fraternity v. George Mason Univ., 993 F.2d 386 (4th Cir. 1993)), many colleges and universities have severely limited the scope of, or completely eliminated, campus speech codes.

In addition to the overbreadth and vagueness doctrines, a third rationale developed by the courts invalidates regulations that are too narrow rather than too broad in scope. In *R.A.V. v. City of St. Paul,* 505 U.S. 377 (1992), the Supreme Court invalidated a city ordinance that made it a misdemeanor to place any symbol or graffiti on public or private property that would arouse anger or resentment on the basis of race, color, creed, religion, or gender. The Court found that the ordinance limited the prohibition of speech to certain viewpoints (i.e., racial, religious, or gender) and ignored hate speech or conduct based on other viewpoints (i.e., political affiliation, union membership, homosexuality). Thus, the Court concluded that the law was unconstitutional because it was underinclusive because it imposed special prohibitions on those speakers who express views on disfavored subjects. Although this rationale is employed less frequently, it has resulted in formation of laws and policies that attempt to list every type of discriminatory viewpoint imaginable.

Limitations on the Exercise of Free Speech

Over time courts have identified certain categories of speech that do not receive First Amendment protection. In those cases, the government may take steps to limit or regulate the content of the prohibited speech, not merely the time, place, or manner in which it is delivered. The categories recognized today are defamation, obscenity and child pornography, and fighting words. Standards for each have evolved through judicial decisions that weighed the free speech mandates of the First Amendment against the societal interest in eliminating such expression.

Standards of Liability

Although speakers clearly enjoy First Amendment protections that limit their liability, they can be civilly or criminally liable to the extent that the expression is not protected. Not only may the individual speaker be liable but under certain circumstances the person or entity that permits the speaker to disseminate the unprotected message may be held legally responsible for the wrong committed. Determining the legal status of the one carrying or repeating the message as a publisher, distributor, or common carrier will determine the standard of liability to which that party is held.

The term *publisher* encompasses all those who communicate statements to third persons or issue a publication. The term includes both the original author and those who subsequently repeat or republish the statement. A party will be characterized as a publisher if it exercises editorial control over a publication. The presumption is that publishers have direct control over what they publish, having at least constructive, if not actual, knowledge of the contents of what is distributed. For instance, a newspaper exerts a high degree of control over the content of its final product. As a result, the Supreme Court determined that the choice of material, decisions as to size and content, and the treatment of public officials constituted enough editorial control and judgment to make the newspaper liable as a culpable party to defamation (Miami Herald Pub'g Co. v. Tornillo, 418 U.S. 241 (1974)).

Publishers have been held liable for stories written by a publisher's employee, letters to the editor, and advertisements. Even though the role of publisher may be clear in print materials, difficulties arise in attaching the publisher analogy to electronic media or broadcasts where the publisher cannot control the input from third parties (see Johnson & Marks, 1993).

A distributor is typically one who delivers or transmits information but does not control the content of a publication. Unlike a publisher, a distributor plays a passive role in receiving or passing along information; consequently, it must have actual knowledge of the defamatory or obscene content of a publication before it will be held liable. Furthermore, if the distributor reasonably believes that the original author is privileged to publish the defamatory material, liability will not attach to the distributor for republishing it.

The concept of a common carrier has developed through both statutory and common law schemes. Unlike publishers or distributors, common carriers have a duty to carry all content, without discrimination, for anyone willing to pay the cost. Because of their indiscriminate nature, common carriers have immunity from liability for what they carry or transmit. An underlying rationale for the limitation on liability is that common carriers have limited rights to inspect or disclose the content of messages on their systems.

It is evident that the legal metaphor—defendant as publisher, distributor, or common carrier—imposed by the courts is critical in the determination of liability in litigation arising out of unprotected speech. The applicability of the traditional analyses in the electronic forum already has been tested by the courts with differing results and implications for access providers.

Defamation

Defamation is a tort involving scandalous words that can be written (libel) or spoken (slander) that damage another's reputation. Although the requirements for defamation may vary from one state to another based on their common law traditions, defamation generally will be found where there is a published or communicated false statement concerning another that brings hatred, disgrace, ridicule, or contempt to the person and results in damage to that person.

Two early cases involving defamation over the Internet had inimical results. In *Cubby* v. *CompuServe*, 776 F. Supp. 135 (S.D.N.Y. 1991), a New York district court considered a case arising out of an alleged defamatory statement made in a publication carried on a computerized database. The facts of the case established that defendant CompuServe developed an electronic library that subscribers could access from a personal computer. CompuServe contracted with an unrelated company to manage and edit the information available in that library. According to the contract, the contents of the library were to conform to the editorial and technical standards established by CompuServe. One of the publications available was a daily newsletter about people in broadcast journalism created by a third company, which directly contracted with the managing company, not CompuServe. CompuServe did not review the contents of the publication before it was uploaded into CompuServe's computer banks.

In 1990 the daily newsletter allegedly posted some defamatory statements about a competitor. The competitor filed suit, including

CompuServe as a defendant. The court determined that CompuServe was not a publisher of the information contained in the newsletter because, although it could decline to carry a publication altogether, CompuServe did not have editorial control over the publication. The court likened Compuserve's product to a traditional library that carried a vast number of publications. Consequently, CompuServe's status was that of a distributor and as such would have to have actual or constructive knowledge of the defamatory statements as a prerequisite to a finding of liability.

In 1995 another provider of news products and services attempted to rely on *Cubby* in a case involving a similar set of facts. In *Stratton Oakmont, Inc. v. Prodigy Services Co.*, 1995 N.Y. Misc. LEXIS 229 (Sup. Ct. N.Y. 1995), a New York state court heard a libel suit for alleged defamatory statements that were posted to the defendant's bulletin board service where subscribers could post statements regarding stocks, investments, and other financial matters. Defendant Prodigy contracted with various individuals to act as discussion leaders and to undertake promotional efforts.

After an unidentified party posted a series of statements to the service accusing the plaintiffs of fraudulent and criminal activity, suit was brought against Prodigy since it was the service provider. The issue before the court was whether Prodigy was a publisher for the purpose of imputing liability for those statements. The court determined that Prodigy held itself out as an on-line service provider that exercised editorial control over the content of the messages that appeared on its bulletin board. In one piece of literature, Prodigy expressly analogized its position to that of a newspaper editor. Moreover, there was additional evidence that Prodigy promulgated content guidelines for its users, employed software to prescreen for offensive language, and provided its leaders with an emergency delete function to remove messages. Based on the level of content control exercised by Prodigy, the court distinguished the holding from *CompuServe*: "Prodigy's conscious choice, to gain the benefits of editorial control, has opened it up to a greater liability than CompuServe and other computer networks that make no such choice" (1995 N.Y. Misc. LEXIS 229, at *13). The court went on to opine that the market would compensate a network for its increased control and resultant increased liability.

Obscenity

A second form of proscribable speech is obscenity. While concerns over obscenity date back to colonial times, the concept always has been a problematic one for the courts and legislatures as the result of the lack of a uniform, workable definition of what constitutes obscenity. The current criteria used to define obscenity were developed by the Supreme Court in the case of *Miller* v. *California*, 413 U.S. 15 (1973). A three-part test was articulated: first, the average person, applying contemporary community standards would find that the work, taken as a whole, appeals to prurient interest; second, the work must depict or describe, in a patently offensive way, sexual conduct specifically defined by the applicable state law; and third, the work, taken as a whole, must lack serious literary, artistic, political, or scientific value. Subsequent cases have all been decided under the *Miller* standard.

Transmitting obscenity via computer networks can result in both criminal and civil liability. The first Internet obscenity case involved a criminal conviction of a California couple, Robert and Carleen Thomas, by a jury in Memphis, Tennessee (United States v. Thomas, 74 F.3d 701 (6th Cir. 1996)). The Thomases operated a bulletin board system (BBS) that provided subscribers with access to sexually explicit pictures for viewing and downloading. The defendants purchased magazines from adult bookstores in California and scanned the pictures into files that were then uploaded to the BBS. There were approximately fourteen thousand images depicting bestiality, oral sex, incest, sadomasochistic abuse, and sex scenes involving urination. The defendants restricted access to the images by issuing passwords to subscribers after they had paid the membership fee and submitted a signed application that required disclosure of the applicant's name, address, age, and telephone number. In addition, the defendants offered adult videotapes for sale via the BBS.

After a U.S. postal inspector in Tennessee paid the subscription fee and downloaded sexually explicit files, the defendants were indicted by a federal grand jury in Tennessee and convicted on eleven counts of interstate transmission and transportation of obscenity that resulted in prison terms for the defendants and seizure of their computer equipment.

On appeal, the primary issue before the Sixth Circuit was whether Tennessee was the proper venue to prosecute the defendants since that was the place where the transmission was received rather than where it originated. The basis of the defendants' argument was that because obscenity is defined by community standards, subjecting the defendants to prosecution for obscenity in Tennessee, which had a less tolerant standard than California was improper. The appellate court upheld the conviction, noting that the defendants had methods in place to limit user access in jurisdictions where the risk of finding obscenity was greater than in California. Because they knew the prospective subscriber's address from the application, the defendants could have refused to issue passwords to users in those jurisdictions, thereby limiting their exposure to liability.

The *Thomas* case is illustrative, not only of the ease with which obscenity can be transmitted nationally or even globally, but of the critical legal ramifications that may accompany a transmission acceptable perhaps in one community but not in another. Taken to an extreme, the government could choose to prosecute Internet obscenity cases in the forum most likely to ensure victory as long as courts follow the community standard test in determining what is obscene.

Another case of Internet obscenity involved detailed written accounts of fantasies about rape, sodomy, and mutilation of a college student. Abraham Alkhabaz, also known as Jake Baker, was an undergraduate student at the University of Michigan. University officials were notified by a university alumnus that the defendant was communicating with an unidentified individual through a series of e-mail exchanges in which he described in lurid detail abducting, abusing, and murdering a named female classmate. Baker also posted a story to the alt.sex.stories newsgroup describing the torture, rape, and murder of the same woman.

Thereafter, university security obtained a written waiver to search Baker's residence and e-mail account. Baker was suspended from the university and subsequently arrested for engaging in interstate communications containing threats to kidnap or injure another person. The district court dismissed the indictment against Baker, reasoning that the e-mail messages sent by Baker did not constitute true threats under the First Amendment and, as such, were protected speech.

On appeal, the Sixth Circuit affirmed the decision of the lower court, finding that the communications between Baker and the unidentified person did not constitute a threat. The two-pronged test imposed by the court was whether a reasonable person (1) would take the statement as a serious expression of an intention to do bodily harm, and (2) would perceive that such expression was being communicated to achieve some goal through intimidation. Even if the facts in *Baker* met the first prong of the test, the court concluded there was no evidence to suggest that Baker was trying to intimidate his unnamed friend to help him carry out his plan. Instead, the court's perception was that the two individuals were sending the e-mail messages in an attempt to "foster a friendship based on shared sexual fantasies." (United States v. Alkhabaz, 104 F.3d 1492, 1497, n.1 (6th Cir. 1997)). Despite repeated attempts by the government to hold the defendant culpable for his Internet activities, the repercussions were limited to dismissal by the institution.

Child Pornography

Child pornography, whether obscene or not, has not received any protection under the First Amendment. The courts have consistently held that states have greater latitude in protecting children as an audience for pornographic material and in preventing sexual exploitation of children in pornographic materials. Courts have upheld convictions under state statutes for the sale of "girlie magazines" to a sixteen-year-old (Ginsberg v. New York, 390 U.S. 629 (1968)); for selling films showing children masturbating (New York v. Ferber, 458 U.S. 747 (1982)); for interstate transportation of child pornography (United States v. X-citement Video, 513 U.S. 64 (1994)); and for possessing or viewing materials that depicted nude children by anyone other than the parent of the child (Osborne v. Ohio, 495 U.S. 103 (1990)).

It is clear from recent cases that the courts have no greater tolerance for child pornography in cyberspace. The existence of computer images deemed to be child pornography on an individual's hard drive was sufficient for a criminal conviction in *United States v. Stevens*, 1998 U.S. Dist. LEXIS 19471, No. A97-0121 CR (D.C. Alaska, Dec. 8, 1998). In that case, a forty-seven-year-old unmarried man with no children was criminally charged for having child pornography images on his hard drive, which were discovered during a routine computer repair. On inspection, several files containing over four hundred images were detected that depicted children engaged in bestiality, sadomasochistic activities, and sex with adults. All of the images on the defendant's computer were obtained through chat rooms on America Online to which the defendant subscribed.

The defendant was convicted under federal law that prohibits a person from possessing a computer disk that contains three or more images of child pornography that has been transported in interstate commerce, including computer transmissions (18 U.S.C. § 2252A(a)(5)(B) (1998)). Although the court upheld a reduction in the maximum sentence allowable under the statute, the defendant, who had never had a criminal record, served a twelve-month prison sentence and was fined $10,000.

Similarly, an FBI investigation of child pornography on the Internet resulted in the indictment of an Ohio individual for transmitting child pornography (United States v. Charbonneau, 979 F. Supp. 1177 (S.D. Ohio 1997)). In that case, an FBI agent, using a screen name, frequented chat rooms known as "BOYS" and "PRETEEN" on America Online (AOL). Although the agent did not actively participate in conversations that took place in the chat room, he sat in the room as an observer. Other users would identify all users in the room and then forward e-mails to each of them, attaching graphic files containing child pornography. The defendant was identified as one of the users sending the pornographic images. The FBI obtained access to the defendant's residence and recovered two computers and a number of disks containing child pornography. The district court summarily dismissed the defendant's claims of First Amendment violations as meritless, although it did recognize that some improprieties existed with respect to the search itself (*id.* at 1184).

Unquestionably, having child pornography on one's computer has serious consequences. In one case a man was fined and sentenced to community service for downloading child pornography from the Internet. In addition, the court ordered him to register as a sex offender as a result of that conviction (Burke, 1995). For college students about to embark on careers, such a record could be devastating.

Fighting Words

Fighting words are those that not only incite anger but do so to such a degree that they cause a breach of the peace. The Supreme Court has repeatedly emphasized that the fighting words doctrine did not reach all offensive language but was limited to speech that had a direct tendency to cause acts of violence by the person to whom the speech was directed (Gooding v. Wilson, 495 U.S. 518, 523 (1972)). As a consequence, the term *fighting words* is interpreted to mean words spoken in a face-to-face confrontation that is likely to create a breach of the peace. To date, no cases have dealt with the issue of fighting words in the Internet context.

Commercial Speech

Although early judicial decisions had concluded that commercial expression was unprotected, by 1975 the Supreme Court resolved that advertising was not stripped of First Amendment protection solely because of its commercial nature (Bigelow v. Virginia, 421 U.S. 809 (1975)). In subsequent cases the Court found that the public had a strong interest in the free flow of commercial information, and it enunciated a four-part test for determining whether a given regulation of commercial speech violates the First Amendment. Restrictions on commercial speech will be upheld only when (1) the commercial speech falls into an unprotected category because it is misleading or concerns an unlawful activity; (2) the government has a substantial interest in regulating the speech; (3) the regulation directly advances the substantial governmental interest; and (4) the regulation is not more extensive than necessary to serve the government's interest (Central Hudson Gas & Elec. v. Public Service Comm'n, 447 U. S. 557 (1980)). Thus, on the continuum of First Amendment protection, commercial speech receives less protection than personal or political expression but greater protection than defamation, obscenity, or fighting words. The difficulty is that the exact amount of protection is unknown because it is based on a case-by-case analysis. Consequently, institutions implementing regulations of commercial speech may not be assured of their validity absent a challenge in court.

The Internet has provided a new venue for commercial speech to occur. As a result, courts have already been confronted with determining the level of First Amendment protection that commercial speech will receive in cyberspace. These judicial decisions may be important for higher education institutions whose network users have the technical ability to engage in commercial activity or may be the target of the commercial speech of others.

A federal district court in Pennsylvania heard the case of *Cyber Promotions v. America Online*, 948 F. Supp. 436 (E.D. Pa. 1996), which presented two novel issues: whether, under the First Amendment, one private company had the right to send unsolicited e-mail advertisements to the subscribers of another company; and whether a private service provider has the right to block the unwanted e-mail advertisements.

In that case, plaintiff Cyber Promotions provided on-line advertising services that resulted in millions of messages to AOL's subscribers on a daily basis, causing an overload of AOL's e-mail servers and angry letters from disgruntled subscribers. After AOL sent a letter to the plaintiff expressing its dissatisfaction with the e-mail advertising, it then sent a number of "e-mail bombs." Defendant AOL gathered all the unsolicited e-mail sent by plaintiff to undeliverable AOL addresses, altered the return path of the plaintiff's e-mail, and then sent the altered e-mail in a bulk transmission back to the plaintiff's service provider, which caused a disruption of network service. The service provider ultimately canceled the plaintiff's subscription to the service.

The district court determined that the plaintiff was unable to prevail on its claim that its right to send e-mail was guaranteed under the First Amendment. The court reasoned that AOL's e-mail system was privately owned; hence, the operation of a computer network did not equate to state action, nor did AOL exercise any powers that were the exclusive prerogative of the state. Despite the fact that AOL had technically opened its e-mail system to the public by connecting to the Internet, it was not performing any municipal function or public service; therefore, AOL was not a state actor. Accordingly, the First Amendment claims were not applicable to AOL. In addition, the court determined that the plaintiff's claims under the state constitution were also without merit as AOL had never presented its e-mail servers to the public at large for dissemination of messages, political or otherwise. America Online's e-mail system was available only to subscribers of AOL and was not a public forum.

In a similar case, *CompuServe v. Cyber Promotions, Inc.*, 962 F. Supp. 1015 (S.D. Ohio 1997), an Ohio district court revisited the First Amendment issue when it dealt with the right of a service provider to prevent a commercial enterprise from sending unsolicited electronic mail to its subscribers. In that case, CompuServe had made several attempts to block the e-mail advertising, but Cyber Promotions was able to circumvent the technology in each instance.

Unable to achieve its goals through electronic means, plaintiff CompuServe filed its complaint in federal court (based on diversity of citizenship), claiming that the continual e-mail advertisements constituted a trespass on its computer network. The primary defense asserted by Cyber Promotions was that the e-mail advertising was protected under the First Amendment. The court relied on the earlier *Cyber Promotions* decision in finding that the plaintiff's service provider was a private entity and not bound by the First Amendment. Under the court's analysis, the actions of defendant Cyber Promotions did constitute actionable trespass under state law because its intentional use of the plaintiff's computer equipment exceeded the plaintiff's consent and continued even after repeated demands to stop. Finally, the court concluded that public interest would not be served by allowing unsolicited e-mail: "It is ironic that if defendants were to prevail on their First Amendment arguments, the viability of electronic mail as an effective means of communication for the rest of society would be put at risk" (*id.* at 1028).

As in traditional environments, the courts seem unwilling to provide commercial speech with the same level of protection as personal speech even if the speech is occurring electronically.

Statutes Affecting Speech

Given the difficulty in drafting legislation that can survive a First Amendment challenge, legislators are often reluctant to enter into the realm of legislating appropriate or decent speech. Yet growing concern over obscene communications or pornographic materials available to users of the Internet, particularly children, brought about the inclusion of the Communications Decency Act (CDA) in the Telecommunications Act of 1996 (Pub. L. No. 104-104 (1996)).

Communications Decency Act

Two separate provisions of the enacted version of the CDA (1) criminally prohibited anyone from knowingly transmitting obscene or indecent communications to any recipient under eighteen years of age (hereafter referred to as section 223(a)) and (2) criminally prohibited the knowing use of an interactive computer service to send a specific person under eighteen years of age, or to display in a manner available to persons under eighteen, communications that depict or describe, in "patently offensive" terms (as measured by contemporary community standards), sexual or excretory activities or organs (hereafter referred to as section 223(d)). (*See* 47 U.S.C. § 223(a) and (d) (1996).) Violators of the CDA would face up to two years in prison for each offense. However, the law did provide affirmative defenses for those who took reasonable good-faith efforts to restrict access by minors to prohibited communication or restricted such access by requiring verification of age (47 U.S.C. § 223(e)(5) (1996)).

Although the CDA was passed in both the House and Senate by a wide margin, multiple plaintiffs, including organizations and individuals involved in computer communication industries and citizen groups, immediately filed lawsuits challenging the constitutionality of section 223 (a) and (d). The case was appealed directly to the Supreme Court under an expedited review process established in the CDA.

ACLU v. *Reno*

One commentator remarked that March 19, 1997—the date on which oral argument was held in *ACLU* v. *Reno*, 521 U.S. 844, (1997)—was the date on which the U. S. Supreme Court "officially met the Internet" (O'Neil, 1997). At issue were the provisions of the CDA that made it a crime to post indecent materials where minors could access them. Equally important, the case also provided the opportunity for the Court to determine the legal nature of the Internet and the degree to which electronic communications resembled other types of protected expression.

The Supreme Court ultimately held that section 223(a) and (d) of the CDA abridged the freedom of speech protected by the First Amendment and were therefore unconstitutional. The Court recognized the legitimacy and importance of the governmental goal of protecting children from harmful materials. It also acknowledged the proliferation of sexually explicit materials available on the Internet that ranged from "modestly titillating to the hardest core" (117 S. Ct. 2329, 2336 (1997)), which could be accessed in the same manner as any other information, either deliberately or unintentionally. Despite the compelling interest of the government, however, the Court concluded that the CDA was not narrowly tailored, thereby suppressing speech that adults were constitutionally entitled to send and receive. (For an analysis of narrow tailoring, see Sable Communications of Cal. v. FCC, 492 U.S. 115 (1989), in which the Court held that sexual expression that is indecent but not obscene is within adults' free speech rights.)

Section 230

Notwithstanding the sound rejection of section 223 (a) and (d) of the CDA by the Supreme Court, other clauses of the CDA operate as law and have had profound ramifications for service providers.

The provision that warrants particular attention is section 230(c)(1), which provides in pertinent part that "no provider or user of an interactive computer service shall be treated as the publisher or speaker of any information provided by another information content provider" (47 U.S.C. § 230(c)(1) (1998)). Under the statute, an interactive computer service is defined as "any information service [or] system . . . that . . . enables computer access by multiple users to a computer server, including . . . such systems operated or services offered by educational institutions" (47 U.S.C. § 230(e)(2) (1998) (emphasis added)).

On its face, this provision appears to exempt service providers from liability for defamatory transmissions over their networks, regardless of any prior knowledge the service provider may have had of the existence of the defamation. Furthermore, section 230 prohibits any state from imposing any liability inconsistent with this provision of the CDA. In short, section 230 bars defamation and other tort actions that might be brought against interactive computer service providers for injury caused by material transmitted by users or any other third persons via the network.

Section 230 may also insulate service providers from civil liability for impinging on free speech under certain circumstances. That provision shields providers and users of interactive computer services from liability for good-faith efforts to restrict access or availability of material that the provider considers to be "obscene, lewd, lascivious, filthy, excessively violent, harassing, or otherwise objectionable, whether or not such material is constitutionally protected" (47 U.S.C. § 230(c)(2)(A) (1998)).

In the 1997 case of *Zeran v. America Online, Inc.*, 129 F.3d 327 (4th Cir. 1997), the Fourth Circuit had the opportunity to review a defamation case against a service provider in light of section 230 provisions. The case arose out of a posting by an unidentified party on an AOL bulletin board advertising "Naughty Oklahoma T-Shirts." The posting described the sale of shirts that bore tasteless and offensive references to the bombing of the federal building in Oklahoma City, which had occurred only a few days earlier. The posting advised that those interested in the shirts should call plaintiff Zeran and included Zeran's home telephone number in Seattle, Washington. As a result, the plaintiff received numerous angry and derogatory calls, including several death threats. Zeran contacted AOL and was assured that the posting would be removed, but AOL would not agree to post a retraction as a matter of policy. The anonymous postings continued over a period of several days, and the threats against Zeran's life escalated to the point where he was put under police protection. Almost two weeks elapsed before an Oklahoma City newspaper published a story exposing the hoax.

Zeran filed suit against AOL, alleging that AOL unreasonably delayed removing the defamatory messages, refused to post retractions, and failed to screen for similar postings after it had been notified. AOL interposed section 230 as an affirmative defense to the plaintiff's complaint and the district court granted a judgment in favor of AOL.

The Fourth Circuit interpreted section 230 as precluding courts from entertaining claims that would place a computer service provider in the role of a publisher; that is, for exercising such editorial functions as deciding whether to publish, withdraw, or postpone content. Plaintiff Zeran argued that section 230 only eliminated publisher status for service providers, thereby leaving liability for being a distributor intact. The court disagreed, noting the practical implications of such a decision: "If computer service providers were subject to distributor liability, they would face potential liability each time they receive notice of a potentially defamatory statement—from any party, concerning any message. Each notification would require a careful yet rapid investigation . . ., a legal judgment . . ., and an on-the-spot editorial decision" (*id.* at 333). In the face of such an onerous burden, service providers would be inclined to remove messages on notification, whether defamatory or not. The impact of the removal, concluded the court, would have a chilling effect on free speech.

In a civil case, a Florida state court found that Section 230 immunized AOL from liability under state negligence law for allowing child pornography to be sold on its system. In *Doe v. America Online*, 1998 Fla. App. LEXIS 1284, No. CL 97-631 AE (1998), the plaintiff sued on behalf of her eleven-year-old son who had been videotaped while engaging in sexual activity with two other minors by another defendant, Richard Lee Russell. Russell then advertised the availability of the tape via AOL and eventually sold a copy to a person he had contacted through AOL. The complaint alleged negligence and violation of Florida law. AOL moved to dismiss the case, citing section 230 as a defense to a claim of state tort liability.

The court agreed that the provision of the CDA shielded AOL from liability because the material was posted by a subscriber. In addition, the court relied on the holding in *Zeran* to determine that

AOL was not liable either as a publisher or a distributor. This court reasoned that the defendant service provider was analogous to a common carrier such as a telephone company that carries communications from numerous third parties; holding otherwise would require AOL to monitor and censor huge volumes of information that are transmitted over its system. The judge concluded that finding AOL liable under these circumstances would undermine the purpose of section 230, which was to encourage on-line service providers to screen for offensive or illegal content without fear of publisher liability.

Case law to date indicates that service providers may rely on section 230 with some degree of certainty in defamation claims arising out of postings by third parties, even if there was a contractual relationship between the service provider and the third party. Given the number of cases arising on the Internet and the perceived deep pockets of commercial service providers, the courts are likely to refine and narrow the circumstances under which section 230 totally exempts service providers from liability.

While initial court rulings appear to uphold the validity of section 230, it is not clear whether a service provider will be immunized from liability if it makes a conscious decision not to remove defamatory material from the system once it is aware of it. Arguably, ownership of the material initially provided by a third party may be imputed to the service provider, rendering section 230 inapplicable. In addition, service providers must be aware that section 230 expressly rejects immunity in the intellectual property area; nor does it permit immunity for criminal violations, including antitrust conspiracy laws (see Tenenbaum, 1998).

Harassment on the Internet

To this point, the discussion has revolved around the fundamental right to free speech, the traditional limitations on speech that have evolved, and the application of those principles to a new medium of communication. These issues are further complicated when the provider of a computer network is also the employer of, or provides educational services to, its network users. Those roles place an affirmative duty on the administrators of a network to prohibit discrimination in accordance with federal law. Conflict may arise when electronic "speech," which is not proscribable, nevertheless creates a hostile or offensive environment for a particular class of users. Internet speech can be discriminatory on ethnic, racial, or religious grounds; however, in light of the proliferation of sexual material available, a dominant concern appears to be sexual harassment. (*See, e.g.*, McGraw, 1995; Oldenkamp, 1997.)

Title VI of the Civil Rights Act (20 U.S.C. §§ 2000(d) *et seq.* (1998)) and title IX of the Education Amendments of 1972 (20 U.S.C. §§ 1681 *et seq.* (1998)) attempt to eradicate race and sex discrimination by educational institutions, including colleges and universities. Both public and private educational institutions may be subject to the mandates of titles VI and IX if they receive federal funding (in 1998, over 95 percent of all public and private institutions received federal financial assistance, according to a recent estimate by HEATH Resources, American Council on Education).

Title IX prohibits sexual discrimination in any aspect of an institution's operations, including all academic, athletic, extracurricular, and other programs of the school, regardless of where they occur. This mandate would presumably include the operation of a campus computer network. Gender-based harassment does not necessarily have to be of a sexual nature; it may include activity that is violent, intimidating, or aggressive if it is based on sex. However, title IX will be violated only if the conduct is of a severe, persistent, or pervasive nature. In deciding whether conduct meets the standard, the courts will look at both subjective and objective factors. Consequently, the alleged victim must perceive the conduct as abusive; in addition, it must be determined that a reasonable person would also perceive the conduct as abusive. In most cases, a hostile environment will be found to exist if there is a pattern or practice of harassment or if the harassment is sustained and not trivial (Office for Civil Rights, Sexual Harassment Guidance: Harassment of Students By School Employees, Other Students, or Third Parties, 62 Fed. Reg. 12,034, 12,038 (1997)).

In addition, sexual conduct must be unwelcome in order to be actionable as harassment. Conduct will generally be unwelcome if the student did not request or invite it and regarded it as undesirable or offensive. Failure to react or act on the conduct does not mean the conduct is welcome; moreover, the fact that the victim may have participated in the conduct on another occasion does not prevent him or her from finding the conduct unwelcome at a later time.

An institution will be liable for harassment by a student's peers or other third parties only if (1) a hostile environment exists in the school's programs or activities, (2) the school knows, or should have known, of the harassment, and (3) the school fails to take immediate and appropriate corrective action. The Supreme Court has recently announced that educational institutions may be held liable for peer-to-peer sexual harassment (see Davis v. Monroe County Bd. of Educ., 119 S. Ct. 1661 (1999)).

An institution will be in violation of title IX if the school has actual or constructive notice that the harassment is taking place. Actual notice occurs when an employee or agent of the institution is informed of the conduct, either directly (i.e., complaint by victim) or indirectly (i.e., school staff, media, member of community). Constructive notice exists if the institution should have known about the harassing activity even though it may not have been aware of it. For instance, if the administration was informed of some incidents of harassment, it is responsible for investigating the possibility of similar incidents. Such a finding by a court would be on the particular facts presented in a case; therefore, such a determination defies application of any bright line standard against which constructive notice can be measured. If the harassing conduct is widespread and public so as to be generally known in the educational community, constructive notice may be imputed to the administration.

Finally, if an institution determines that sexual harassment has occurred, it needs to take prompt remedial action to avoid liability. The corrective action needs to be reasonable, timely, and appropriate to end the harassment. Moreover, the institution should implement measures to prevent recurrences of the harassing conduct or retaliation against the complaining party. Should the institution fail to demonstrate that it adequately responded to the harassing situation when it was obligated to do so, it will incur liability.

This brief overview of the requirements of title IX (and, by analogy, titles VI and VII) illustrates the burden placed on the employer or educational institution to prevent harassment within its confines. The introduction of computer networks in the workplace, in schools, and on campuses now takes that obligation a step further. Although these networks open new channels of communication between employees, students, and the rest of the world, they also present another context in which harassment can take place. Sexual harassment may be perpetuated by displaying pornographic images on a computer terminal in common work areas or computer laboratories. E-mail may be a more egregious means by which to harass an individual or group of people.

Computer Pornography

A great deal of sexually explicit material is accessible on the Internet that could be perceived as pornographic, depending on the defining party. In fact, a study several years ago concluded that over 900,000 sexually explicit images were available for downloading on the Internet. These pornographic images include displays of men, women, and children in nude photos engaged in a wide variety of sexual acts, including sadomasochism and pedophilia. The proliferation of this cyberporn has drawn a great deal of interest, particularly from male users (see Rimm, 1995). Even though no restrictions exist on access from home (provided users are the age of majority and have a credit card number), accessing this material in an area of the workplace or educational institution can subject to the display on the computer screen peers who may find it offensive or even intimidating.

Prior judicial decisions have held that the posting of print pictures of nude and partially nude women throughout the workplace substantially contributed to a hostile environment and a finding that female workers had suffered sexual harassment (Harris v. Forklift Sys., 510 U.S. 17 (1993)). By analogy, the display of pornography on a computer terminal that is readily visible to others who are working, standing, or walking nearby may be construed as creating a hostile environment. If the other elements of a sexual harassment claim are established, the employer or educational institution may be liable.

Prohibiting Access to Pornography

In an effort to curtail their users' ability to access on-line pornography, some institutions have instituted policies or implemented technical blocks to sexually explicit sites. Several lawsuits have resulted from the imposition of laws or policies that prevent adult users from accessing pornography on the Internet.

One professor sued the university president for implementing a policy that effectively blocked the professor's access to some newsgroups on the Internet that purportedly carried obscene materials. The professor filed a lawsuit claiming violation of his First Amendment right to free speech. The evidence established that prior to March 1996, users of the Oklahoma University server had unlimited access to all newsgroups on the Internet. After being informed that providing access to certain newsgroups might make the university a distributor of obscene materials in violation of Oklahoma law, the university president-defendant resolved to block access to reputedly obscene newsgroups.

After a trial of the matter, the court found that the new policy met constitutional standards. More important, the court found that the university network did not constitute a public forum for First Amendment purposes as it had never been open to the general public or used for public communications. Consequently, it could be restricted for academic and research purposes. The Tenth Circuit affirmed the district court decision. (*see* Loving v. Boren, 956 F. Supp. 953 (W.D. Okla. 1997), *aff'd*, 133 F.3d 771 (10th Cir. 1998)).

In another higher education setting, several professors at Virginia state colleges and universities filed a lawsuit challenging the constitutionality of a state statute that restricted the ability of state employees to access sexually explicit material on state-owned or leased computers. In *Urofsky v. Gilmore*, 167 F.3d 191 (4th Cir. 1999), the plaintiffs claimed that the law unconstitutionally interfered with their research and teaching. For example, one professor claimed he could not assign students on-line research projects concerning indecency laws; another alleged that she had to discontinue her Internet research on gay and lesbian studies; a third claimed an inability to access a database of sexually explicit poetry by Victorian poets.

In examining the standard of review for speech by government employees, the court determined that the employees are entitled to full First Amendment protection when they speak on matters of public concern, whereas matters of private concern (i.e., personal employment grievances) are unprotected. This protection must be balanced against the government's interest in workplace efficiency and hostile work environment claims. However, the district court found that the Virginia statute that was crafted to ameliorate those problems was fatally flawed for three reasons. First, the law was over-inclusive because it categorically restricted all sexually explicit material regardless of work-related endeavors of employees dealing with sexuality or the human body. Second, the statute was underinclusive because it only targeted distractions on the computer that were sexual in nature; it did not prohibit access to on-line video games, chat rooms, or shopping sites that also could result in workplace disruption and have an impact on employee efficiency. Finally, the court found that content-neutral alternatives existed (i.e., restricting computer use solely for the purpose of conducting university business) that would not violate freedom of expression. Accordingly, the Virginia statute was struck down.

On appeal, however, the Fourth Circuit reversed the decision of the district court on narrow grounds. In analyzing the applicable law, the court distinguished between the First Amendment rights of state employees when the speech is made in the employee's role as a citizen, as opposed to speech made in the role of an employee of the government. Based on the court's interpretation of constitutional case law, First Amendment protection extended only to speech made as a citizen and of public concern. The court then determined that the challenged aspect of the Virginia statute regulated only the speech of state employees in their capacity as employees, not their speech as citizens. Under that rationale, the state retained the ability to control and direct the manner in which its employees performed their assigned duties.

The court limited its decision to speech made solely as employees without public concern. In a concurring opinion, one judge stated that "we leave unanswered the question of whether a government employee who seeks to access and disseminate sexually explicit materials rising to the level of matters of public concern, not in his or her role as a governmental employee, but rather as a private citizen, is entitled to some measure of First Amendment protection. The facts of this case leave that issue for another day" (*id.* at 197).

E-Mail Harassment

Numerous incidents of e-mail harassment have occurred on campus networks. Some blame an e-mail protocol that is blunt and direct, given the perceived distance and anonymity in e-mail messaging. For the recipients of unwanted e-mail, the avoidance of harassing messages often is difficult. Although some sophisticated computer systems have software components that permit a user to block all future messages from a sending site (i.e., a "kill" file), most businesses and educational systems do not provide this option. In some instances, the user can delete the unwelcome message without reading it; in others, the system will not permit deletion of a message without its being opened first. Even if the recipient is not forced to read the harassing message in its entirety, the repeated sending of e-mails is akin to telephone calls where the caller simply hangs up when the call is answered, which can be as disturbing as a face-to-face confrontation.

Using technological methods to prevent e-mail harassment is most effective when the sender and the recipient of the e-mails are using a computer system managed by the same system administrator. These technological restraints on use are weaker when e-mail travels from one computer network to another; the recipient would have to contact the system administrator of the sender's system for the sender to be denied access. Even if the system administrator is willing to cooperate in denying access, the sender may find alternative ways to resume sending messages.

If these extralegal methods of stopping e-mail harassment fail, the recipient has possible legal recourse against the sender under a theory of tort liability and under some state stalking statutes. Sexual harassment cases have generally raised three claims based on tort liability: assault, intentional infliction of emotional distress, and invasion of privacy. (For a detailed discussion of these torts, see *Restatement (Second) of Torts* 46 (1965).) In the context of cyberspace, it is improbable that one could prevail on a claim of assault requiring the victim to be apprehensive of immediate physical contact. This theory might not be available in cases where the e-mail sender is in some distant location and could not possibly carry out a threat of physical violence; however, e-mails between workers or classmates in close proximity to one another could create a situation in which a reasonable person is apprehensive of harm.

Intentional infliction of emotional distress has been used in sexual harassment cases where the harassing conduct is "extreme and outrageous," and intentionally or recklessly causes severe emotional distress to the victim (Samms v. Eccles, 358 P. 2d 344 (Utah 1961)). Generally, the courts have set a fairly high standard for what constitutes outrageous behavior; however, that determination is made by a court on a case-by-case basis on the circumstances presented. For example, a man who persistently telephoned a woman over a period of eight months asking her to have sexual intercourse was held liable for intentional infliction of emotional distress. The court found that the solicitation for intercourse would, under ordinary circumstances, be considered offensive. Given the period of time over which it continued, however, this activity created emotional distress and warranted recovery (see, Prosser, 1971).

A third tort that may be applicable is invasion of privacy. To prevail on an action for invasion of privacy, the plaintiff needs to establish that the nature of the intrusion would be offensive or objectionable to a reasonable person (Rogers v. Loew's Enfant Plaza Hotel, 526 F. Supp. 523 (D.D.C. 1981)). This theory has been used successfully in cases against bill collectors who used the telephone and mailings to harass debtors. Similarly, this theory has been used as a means of recovery in sexual harassment cases where the harassment occurred by telephone. To the extent that e-mail is found analogous to telephone calls, the tort of invasion of privacy may also provide an additional avenue of relief for victims of computer harassment.

Most states have stalking laws that make it a criminal offense to engage in conduct that places the victim in reasonable fear of death or bodily injury or causes severe emotional distress. Although the specific requirements and definitions vary by state, most stalking laws proscribe threatening behavior that takes place over a period of time. The use of stalking laws to prosecute for unwanted e-mail was tested in Michigan when a couple who met through a computer dating service corresponded by e-mail for several days before the woman terminated the cyberspace romance. The defendant continued to e-mail her, even after the police notified him to desist from communicating with the woman. The defendant was ultimately charged with violating the state stalking law and was found guilty (Durfee, 1996.)

Although the foregoing illustrates possible legal ramifications for the perpetrator of harassing e-mail messages, there also may be liability on the part of the provider of the system that carries the offending communications under the federal laws proscribing harassment. As noted previously, the employer or educational institution that knows or should have known of the harassing e-mail and does not take appropriate measures to remedy the situation is likely to be held responsible for the existence of a hostile environment. Whether an institution will be held liable for sexual harassment will depend on the severity and duration of the harassing e-mail. For example, a single incident of racist e-mail, standing alone, will not lead a court to find the prerequisite hostile environment (Owens v. Morgan Stanley & Co., 1997 U.S. Dist. LEXIS 10351 (S.D.N.Y. 1997)). An institution's standard of duty required in such a circumstance has yet to be resolved, especially as Congress has placed limitations on the extent to which electronic communications can be monitored. Until some of these incidents make their way through the judicial system, the courts' disposition regarding the level of safeguards necessary to prevent harassment is purely speculation.

Implications for Higher Education

Notwithstanding the growing presence of computer systems on campuses, the university has no legal obligation to provide access to a network. Once a computer network is provided, however, certain legal obligations arise with respect to speech that takes place in that medium, particularly on the part of publicly supported colleges and universities.

Academic Freedom

Academic freedom is a special concern of higher education institutions; it provides a higher level of deference to speech than that afforded by the Constitution. Even though a precise definition of academic freedom is elusive, the U.S. Supreme Court has confirmed that "[a]cademic freedom thrives not only on the independent and uninhibited exchange of ideas among teachers and students . . . but also, and somewhat inconsistently, on autonomous decision making by the academy itself" (Regents of the University of Michigan v. Ewing, 474 U.S. 214, 2226 n.12 (1985)).

Although the legal boundaries of academic freedom are initially defined by contract in all institutions of higher education, public colleges and universities are also bound by constitutional concepts of academic freedom. These constitutional concepts have been developing since the 1950s when the Supreme Court gave academic freedom constitutional status under the First Amendment freedoms of speech and association. Whereas the earlier cases focused on a faculty member's right to refuse to sign a loyalty oath and the right to maintain membership in various associations, later decisions affirmed the right of faculty to speak out on matters of public concern, irrespective of whether the forum in which the speech took place was public or private. Moreover, academic freedoms clearly extend to research and publication activities of faculty members (Levin v. Harleston, 770 F. Supp. 895, aff'd, 966 F.2d 85 (2d Cir. 1992)). However, the courts have always balanced an individual's academic freedom against the right of the institution to maintain an efficient educational system (Pickering v. Board of Educ., 391 U.S. 563 (1968); Connick v. Myers, 461 U.S. 138 (1983); Givhan v. Western Line Consolidated Sch. Dist., 439 U.S. 410 (1979)).

Judicial decisions regarding academic freedom are numerous, often conflicting, and well beyond the scope of this book. Nevertheless, one conclusion is obvious: administrators' authority to limit academic freedom carries with it certain restrictions.

Electronic communications, notably e-mail, greatly expand opportunities to exercise academic freedom. Preventing open exchanges of information, even if well intentioned, may bring challenges based on academic freedom. For example, an institution that uses filtering software to prevent access to Web sites using the word *skin* on the college's Web browser in an attempt to block out sexually explicit materials may simultaneously prevent a biology professor from accessing legitimate scientific information (*see* Franke & Michelson, 1999). Thus, the institution must consider the academic freedom of its faculty when determining the speech to be tolerated on campus computer networks as well as the materials readily accessed in that forum. Most institutions have in place their own guidelines on academic freedom and internal systems for protecting academic freedom in accordance with institutional policy. Caution must be exercised in the development of computer use policies that are sensitive to contractual or constitutional guarantees of academic freedom. This is not to imply, however, that the institution must forgo regulation of its computer network for fear of trampling an individual's academic freedom. Legitimate institutional educational goals should take precedence.

Reasonable Limitations

The threshold obligation is to allow free expression in keeping with the spirit of the First Amendment. Although primary and secondary schools may have legitimate concerns over the content of speech to which its students are exposed, higher education has primarily an adult population. Restrictions on speech appropriate in the K–12 setting will not be justified at this level.

The fact that the content of speech may not be regulated, however, does not prevent the institution from imposing reasonable limitations on the time, place, and manner of the speech. Although only one appellate court has expressly determined that a university computer network does not constitute a public forum, that conclusion is likely to be supported because a campus network is open only to members of the university community, not to the general public. Consequently, the institution may implement rules and regulations to guide the time, place, and manner in which network communications take place, provided that the subject matter of the communication is not thereby impacted. For example, a public university may want to provide computer labs with restricted access, while at the same time another lab would not be so restricted. As long as those restrictions are well publicized to users, constitutional challenges would be avoided. In addition, restrictions must be carefully drafted so as not to be overbroad in their scope or too vague to be understood by the student population of the university.

The institution may choose to eliminate network communications that are defamatory or obscene in nature. Those forms of expression are unprotected and the institution incurs no liability under the First Amendment for removing the material from the network. The problem for the institution is in determining what actually is defamatory without conducting an investigation to determine the veracity of the statements. Similarly, determining what is obscene or pornographic under community standards (i.e., proscribable) versus what is sexually explicit (i.e., permissible) can be challenging. The complexities associated with these decisions have led some institutions to take a laissez-faire attitude to the material on campus computer networks.

Section 230 of the CDA is important because it exculpates service providers from tort liability for transmissions instituted by a user or other third party. Although judicial decisions to date have supported total immunity on the basis of the language in section 230, some question remains as to the potential for liability if the access provider leaves the questionable material on the system even after it has been notified of its damaging nature. For those institutions that do undertake the task of monitoring their campus networks, the "good samaritan" provision of section 230 discussed earlier also provides protection for those service providers who voluntarily take action to restrict access to, or availability of, obscene or otherwise objectionable material. It should be noted, however, that this statutory provision conflicts with the general rule of common law wherein the likelihood of liability increases in direct proportion to the degree of control exercised.

It may be prudent for institutions to develop administrative policies that meet the common law threshold, with the statutory protections adding an additional measure of security. For example, a university that is put on notice of a possibly defamatory message probably should take steps to delete the message rather than relying only on section 230 for protection. Likewise, if the institution is monitoring the network, it should delete information only in instances where the material is clearly proscribable.

Despite the fact that fighting words are also not protected by the First Amendment, fighting words, by their current definition, simply may not exist in the electronic environment. As discussed earlier, fighting words are those words that can create an *immediate* breach of the peace. In the context of computer communications, as contrasted with a face-to-face confrontation, an immediate breach of the peace would be highly unlikely (unless the computers were situated in the same room or computer lab). Attempting to regulate or discipline hate speech on computer networks is fraught with the same difficulty as the courts have determined that fighting words are the only form of hate speech whose prohibition will withstand constitutional scrutiny.

Commercial speech on campus networks is subject to regulation. Cases to date have held that networks operated by private commercial entities are not public forums in which commercial speech receives First Amendment protection. Under that rationale, a network operated by an educational institutional for academic and research purposes would be less likely to be considered a forum for commercial speech. Thus, policies banning advertising or solicitation on campus networks would likely be upheld in the courts.

Even though some regulation of speech is permitted under limited circumstances, the university does not have an affirmative duty to censor speech. An exception to this general rule exists, however, when the speech operates to create a hostile environment for an employee or a student. As noted previously, a hostile environment may occur only in common areas of the university, such as computer centers, libraries, science centers, food courts, and lounges. Students who choose to view offensive materials within the confines of their room should be free to do so, provided the material is not obscene or deemed to be child pornography. Moreover, students viewing or reading pornography in certain common areas would not create a hostile environment, provided they do not intentionally or negligently expose unwilling viewers to the pornography. For example, pornographic writing on a computer screen in a computer lab would not be easily readable by other lab users; conversely, pornographic pictures at a computer terminal might not be avoidable by other students as a result of the typically open layout of the room.

To assure that all students have equal access to the common facilities of the institution, thereby avoiding liability for sexual harassment, the university should implement policies that promote the student's free inquiry and expression and restrict it only when it has a negative impact on another student's freedom to learn in a nonhostile setting.

Under title IX regulations, educational institutions are required to adopt and publish a policy against sex discrimination in addition to grievance procedures that provide for a prompt and equitable resolution of complaints (see 34 C.F.R. § 106.8(b) (1997)). In fact, an institution that fails to have those policies and procedures in effect is considered to be in violation of title IX, regardless of whether harassment occurred (62 Fed. Reg. 12,051 (1997)). To meet these mandates, the institution must designate at least one employee to coordinate efforts toward compliance with federal law, including an investigation of complaints. In addition, the institution should provide public notice of its policy against sexual harassment. A conduct code should be prepared and disseminated to the university community outlining the type of physical or verbal conduct that creates a hostile environment. Where possible, the university should avoid the role of disciplinarian, limiting punitive measures to cases of egregious or repeated conduct; lesser offenses could result in an apology or corrective education. (For further discussion, see Oldekamp, 1997.)

The lack of intervention on the part of the university administrators accomplishes several goals; first, it makes the student community more aware of (and perhaps more sensitive to) issues that will continue to present themselves in the workplace. Second, the operation of the grievance process makes the community more responsible for policing itself. Third, the absence of administrative involvement may reduce the risk of raising First Amendment claims against the institution. Finally, the implementation of a timely and efficient grievance mechanism should meet the requirement that the institution take immediate and appropriate corrective action to preclude title IX claims.

Absent specific circumstances that raise discrimination and harassment issues, the university should avoid attempts to regulate speech on its network. The adage that offensive speech should be combated by more speech holds true in the electronic environment. A recent example at Stanford University highlights the effectiveness of this approach. In responding to an incident of racist e-mail, the university defended the sender's right to remain anonymous and responded with its own e-mail message "to repudiate the hateful message this person sent." The anonymous sender of the racist e-mail then sent another e-mail apologizing to the university community for his earlier message (*see* Mangan, 1999).

Based on the foregoing discussion, the answers to questions posed earlier are perhaps more apparent. An institution does not have to provide access to all Internet sites, the fact that it serves an adult population notwithstanding. Despite recurring First Amendment arguments, a campus network is not a public forum. Generally speaking, a university service provider will not be held liable for defamatory on-line remarks of its users, under section 230 of the CDA. With respect to the female student who is receiving sexually harassing e-mails, the network administrator must take immediate steps to prevent the receipt of further e-mails through technological measures, whether the institution is public or private. If the e-mails occur in the context of an on-line course, the network administrator should suspend the sender's account, but the sender should be afforded the appropriate due process afforded in institutional policies, as discussed in Chapter Four.

Recommendations

1. Use clear policy language.

Using simple language rather than esoteric legal terminology promotes understanding. If there is any doubt as to clarity, get feedback from a sample of students, staff, and faculty to determine if they agree on the meaning of select terms or conditions of the policy. Vague policies may increase the possibility of selective and unfair enforcement. Although vagueness standards imposed by the courts are not necessarily the same, it is best to outline and define prohibited on-line activity in the policy to limit First Amendment challenges under the vagueness doctrine. Finally, a policy also will be more understandable if it is succinct. In this context, less is more.

2. Prohibit commercial activity.

Many computer use policies attempt to limit campus network use to purposes related to the university. This has become problematic because what constitutes a university-related purpose is subject to interpretation by the various constituents of the institution. A more acceptable limitation on network use may be to proscribe commercial activity by users or any activity for financial or other gain. This avoids the problem of setting parameters for academic and personal social use while setting definable boundaries. Potential First Amendment problems are also circumvented as commercial speech may be limited when it does not comport with the educational purposes of the institution or the services it provides.

3. Avoid speech regulation.

Acceptable use policies, in the absence of compelling reasons to the contrary, should not attempt to regulate speech on campus networks, particularly in public institutions that have First Amendment concerns. There are numerous reasons to avoid this type of content restriction on electronic communications.

First, the task of constructing content regulations governing speech that can survive a constitutional challenge is formidable. Clearly, there are categories of speech that are proscribable, including defamation, obscenity and pornography, and fighting words. The difficulty arises when administrators attempt to draft appropriate and well-defined language that regulates such speech without creating a policy that is vague, overbroad, or underinclusive in its scope. Moreover, identifying speech that falls into the prohibited categories is equally troublesome. For example, what is obscene or pornographic is largely a matter of interpretation and can vary from one legal jurisdiction to another. In addition, there are criminal statutes in every state that govern illegal transmissions of pornographic materials; these existing laws provide recourse if incidents occur. Defamatory speech exists only if the requisite elements exist in a particular instance. Even prohibiting fighting words would be superfluous in a computer policy because the electronic venue is not conducive to immediately inciteful speech as it would be in a face-to-face confrontation.

Second, section 230 of the CDA immunizes service providers from liability for defamation occurring on its network, provided that the communications are initiated by the users of a system or third parties who transmit over the system. Section 230 has been successfully asserted as a defense by service providers in both federal and state courts. What has not been tested is the extent of immunity section 230 will provide if the service provider allows the material to remain on the system after actual or constructive notice has been received. In any event, removing or censoring material after it has been alleged to be damaging in nature will probably be viewed more favorably by the courts than any prior restriction on speech content.

Third, institutions can restrict access to objectionable material on their networks through technological means. For institutions that choose to use it, filtering or blocking software can be employed to reduce the availability of obscene, excessively violent, or harassing material transmitted over the network. In addition, section 230 shields service providers from liability for good faith efforts to restrict access to material deemed to be inappropriate despite the fact that the material may be constitutionally protected.

Fourth, provided an institution has a policy in effect covering both racial and sexual harassment, there is no need to redefine these concepts again in the computer policy. It would be advisable to amend the sexual harassment policy to include electronic communications if the language contained in the policy is not sufficiently inclusive; otherwise, the acceptable use policy might state that harassment occurring on the network is subject to existing harassment policies, thereby putting users on notice that such activity will be subjected to disciplinary measures.

4. **Include a general statement on civility.**

For those institutions that wish to make reference to or cite appropriate speech in their policies, a general statement regarding the institutional commitment to civility in electronic communications, without attaching sanctions to purported violations, has no First Amendment implications.

Conclusion

Speech appears to have made the transition to cyberspace with its First Amendment protection intact. Consequently, colleges and universities that are bound by the First Amendment, or similar contractual provisions, must tread carefully in attempting to shape communications on campus computer networks. Censorship will be permitted in limited circumstances only; at the same time, other compelling considerations force higher education institutions to walk a fine line between promoting expression and protecting their constituents.

3

Privacy Issues in Electronic Communications

The traditional notion of privacy limited an individual's freedom from intrusion to the sanctity of the individual's person or home. Cyberspace presents a new dilemma for this legal paradigm. Indeed, a computer terminal may be located in one's home or on one's desk, but personal information, once transmitted, has no geographical location; it joins billions of other bytes of information on the Internet. Similarly, communications over computer networks, whether for the benefit of the public (e.g., postings to newsgroups) or those directed to one other person (e.g., e-mail) also pose privacy concerns because they travel over open network lines.

Technological efforts to ensure privacy of transmissions continues to challenge the experts in the field. At the same time, legislators and courts are attempting to determine the level of legal protection these communications realistically can, or ideally should, be afforded.

The resolution of privacy concerns in cyberspace has enormous implications for colleges and universities that provide campus computer networks for their students, faculty, and staff. As noted in earlier chapters, institutions of higher education have multiple roles to fulfill. Each of those roles (e.g., network service provider, employer, educational entity) carries with it legal and ethical responsibilities that require the protection of privacy rights of the individuals in the university community. For public institutions, shielding students and faculty from intrusion may arise from obligations arising under the United States Constitution or federal statute; for private colleges and universities, similar responsibilities may derive from state law or contractual requirements between the institution and the student or faculty member.

At the same time, however, the university has a vested interest in promoting access to information for users of its computer networks. Given that information is a prerequisite for research and the knowledge gained from it, the mission of higher education requires colleges and universities to be in the vanguard of our information society. In addition, considerable resources must be committed to acquiring the technology infrastructure for a campus computer network; in order to realize a return on its investment, institutions must promote maximum use of their systems for research, communication, and even distance learning. It is imperative, therefore, to have policies and practices in place that assure users that their communications and personal information will be protected, while at the same time permitting the university to fulfill its obligations as the system operator and administrator. These dual roles give rise to difficult decisions for system administrators. What, for example, should network administrators do if they receive a request from the FBI for the e-mail of a student suspected of hacking? Or, what legal recourse does the university have against someone hacking into its system?

Individual users must also be aware of the legal consequences of their activity. For instance, what are the legal repercussions for a disgruntled professor hacking into the personnel files of his or her previous institution?

To understand the practical and legal ramifications of privacy on campus computer networks, it is necessary to examine the legal parameters of privacy, including recent statutes and judicial decisions that apply legal precedent to the new technology. Also reviewed are emerging scenarios on campuses that have implications for future policy formation and administration of computer networks.

Constitutional Privacy

The United States Constitution does not expressly protect privacy; nevertheless, courts have considered privacy claims in the context of reproduction (Roe v. Wade, 410 U.S. 113 (1973) and sexuality (Griswold v. Connecticut, 381 U.S. 479, 485 (1965)). Moreover, various interpretations by the Supreme Court find an implied right to privacy in the First Amendment (freedoms of expression and association), the Fourth Amendment (protection against unreasonable searches and seizures), the Fifth Amendment (privilege against self-incrimination), the Ninth Amendment (constitutional rights do not displace other rights), and the Fourteenth Amendment (guarantee of ordered liberty). Privacy in electronic communications has most often given rise to Fourth Amendment arguments.

Fourth Amendment

The Fourth Amendment requires that governmental conduct falling within the constitutional definition of *search* or *seizure* be reasonable. A seizure of property is a "meaningful interference with an individual's possessory interest in that property" (United States v. Jacobsen, 466 U.S. 109, 113 (1984)). In cases where the property is of a tangible nature, simply removing the property from the possession of the individual constitutes a seizure; however, when the property is intangible, the question of interference with possession becomes more difficult.

Clearly, the confiscation of computer equipment would be a seizure; likewise, removing computer data from the actual possession of the individual would also interfere with possession. Whether copying (for the purpose of viewing) an individual's computer files without disturbing the owner's access to the original files will be deemed a seizure of the computer files has not yet been determined. The cases to date have dealt with simultaneous seizure of equipment and files. For example, in *Steve Jackson Games, Inc. v. United States Secret Service*, 816 F. Supp. 432 (W.D. Tex. 1993), federal agents seized three computers and three hundred computer disks in the possession of a criminal suspect in order to review all information and documents in any computer accessible to the suspect.

The constitutional definition of a search under the Fourth Amendment is even more problematic when applied to electronic communications and computer networks. The 1967 Supreme Court decision in *Katz* v. *United States*, 389 U.S. 347 (1967), discarded a traditional area-based analysis for a search and focused instead on the individual's "expectation of privacy" with respect to the object or area that was searched. Since *Katz*, the accepted standard for determining whether a search has occurred requires that two conditions must be met. First, the person must exhibit an actual or subjective expectation of privacy in the object or place searched. Second, the person's expectation must be one that society recognizes as reasonable.

Reasonable Expectation of Privacy

What constitutes a reasonable expectation of privacy under the Fourth Amendment has engendered considerable debate, especially in the electronic environment. To make this determination, the courts have asked whether the individual affected should have expected that he or she would be undisturbed. If one willingly discloses information to another, there can be no reasonable expectation of privacy in the disclosed information. In *Katz*, the Court said that "what a person knowingly exposes to the public . . . is not a subject of Fourth Amendment protection" (389 U.S. at 351). Under this rationale, a person cannot object to government acquisition of any information the person knowingly disseminated to a third party, provided the information is obtained directly from the third party. (*See*, for example, United States v. Miller, 425 U.S. 435, 442 (1976), in which the Court found no privacy interest in bank deposit slips where the information in the deposit slips was disclosed to the bank; and Smith v. Maryland, 442 U.S. 735, 743 (1979), in which the Court held that no privacy interest was included in telephone numbers that were dialed because the numbers were disclosed to the telephone company. For further discussion, see Sergent, 1995.)

The courts have also been reluctant to find a reasonable expectation of privacy in cases of consent. These generally arise when an individual gives control of an item or an area to a third party while still maintaining an expectation of privacy in the item or area. If the third party consents to a search of the item or area while it is in the party's control, there is no violation of the Fourth Amendment (United States v. Matlock, 415 U.S. 164 (1974)). Absent that third-party consent, however, the expectation of privacy remains. By contrast, under the disclosure analysis, the individual would have forfeited the expectation of privacy the moment the information was transferred, irrespective of the willingness of the third party to consent to the search. The distinguishing feature between consent and disclosure seems to be whether the police could have legally conducted the search without consent; if not, then consent principles should apply. Some courts have not made this distinction; for example, in United States v. White, 401 U.S. 745, 749–53 (1971), the monitoring by police of a telephone conversation with the consent of one of the parties was treated as a case of disclosure.

The knowing exposure rationale in Katz has also been used to imply that if something is accessible or visible to the public, it will be deemed to have been knowingly exposed, regardless of the likelihood of the public actually seeing it. For example, there is no privacy interest in garbage bags placed at the curb of a public street (California v. Greenwood, 486 U.S. 35, 40 (1988)), nor was there a violation of the Fourth Amendment when the police conducted an aerial surveillance of a person's backyard (California v. Ciraolo, 476 U.S. 207 (1986)).

This strand of cases has given rise to the "plain view" doctrine in Fourth Amendment law. In Horton v. California, 496 U.S. 128 (1990), the Supreme Court determined that "if an article is already in plain view, neither its observation nor its seizure would involve any invasion of privacy" (id. at 133). Under this doctrine, an official does not violate the Fourth Amendment by a warrantless seizure of property if the item was visible from a legally gained vantage point (i.e., the officer did not violate the Fourth Amendment by accessing that location); however, the incriminating nature of the item has to be "immediately apparent" (*id*. at 136).

Given the judicial exceptions for disclosure, consent, and plain view, it appears that an individual's reasonable expectation of privacy has been severely limited for any personal information previously disclosed by the person.

Standing

Another limitation on the scope of the Fourth Amendment involves the standing of the person disputing the legality of a particular search or seizure. The Supreme Court has adopted the rule that only an individual who is the victim of the search or seizure is permitted to challenge it (Jones v. United States, 362 U.S. 257 (1960)). The test for having standing to challenge a search is the same as that used to determine whether that search falls within the scope of the Fourth Amendment—the individual must establish a reasonable expectation of privacy. This distinction becomes important when a third party is in possession of property belonging to another. Standing may be an issue in cases occurring in cyberspace, where information on an individual's computer may actually be owned by a third party who transmitted the information.

As illustrated above, the Fourth Amendment has been construed to prohibit unreasonable government intrusion in matters in which a person has a reasonable expectation of privacy. The Constitution does not, however, protect citizens from unlawful invasions of their privacy by other private citizens or entities.

Reasonableness of the Search

Even when a reasonable expectation of privacy has been established, the Fourth Amendment does not prohibit all searches and seizures. Rather, the Fourth Amendment prohibits *unreasonable* searches. For criminal searches, reasonableness usually requires probable cause and a warrant. The standards for reasonableness of a search by officials at a public institution are less stringent because most searches are conducted to determine infractions of a student code or workplace malfeasance rather than criminal activity.

Determining the reasonableness of any search involves a two-fold inquiry: (1) whether the action was justified at its inception; and (2) whether the search actually conducted was reasonably related in scope to the circumstances that justified interference in the first place (New Jersey v. T.L.O., 469 U.S. 325 (1985)). Even though the reasonableness of a search is determined on a case-by-case basis, subsequent decisions have established that individualized suspicion is necessary for a constitutionally valid search.

The requirement of individualized suspicion under the Fourth Amendment generally prevents a public employer or institution from conducting random searches, or searching all employees or students. Given these parameters, it is unlikely that a public employer or institution would be able to justify routine e-mail monitoring in the absence of specific circumstances discussed in subsequent sections.

Application to Cyberspace

Many commentators have struggled with predicting the way in which courts will interpret existing Fourth Amendment law in the electronic venue. Any analysis involving computer networks is complicated by the fact that there are multiple users on most computer networks that are owned and operated by third parties. Under those circumstances, it is questionable whether the courts will find that a user can assert a reasonable expectation of privacy in information found on the network, especially when the user does not have ownership or control of the underlying storage media.

One case involving the court-martial of a military officer has implications for the Fourth Amendment's reasonable expectation of privacy standard with respect to e-mail communications. In United States v. Maxwell, 45 M.J. [Military Justice Reporter] 406 (C.M.A. [Court of Military Appeals] 1996), an Air Force colonel was disciplined for distributing obscene materials and transporting or receiving child pornography in interstate commerce. The conviction was appealed to the court of appeals for the armed forces, where the primary issue was whether the search of computer files that produced the offending materials was constitutional.

The evidence presented demonstrated that law enforcement officials began their investigation of the defendant as a result of a tip from an America Online (AOL) subscriber in California to the FBI that child pornography was being distributed on AOL. After producing a warrant to obtain the identity of AOL subscribers using certain screen names, the FBI traced one of the screen names to the colonel (the defendant). A search of the defendant's AOL records extracted e-mail messages with attached graphics files. The matter was then turned over to the Air Force Office of Special Investigations, which seized the defendant's personal computer and subsequently downloaded pornographic images from graphics files located on the computer.

The defendant challenged the constitutionality of the AOL search on the grounds that both the warrant and the search were overly broad and violated the Fourth Amendment. In addition, he challenged the lower court's consideration of the evidence gained from the seizure of his computer, as it was the result of the first illegal search.

In determining the constitutionality of the AOL search, the court found that AOL e-mail messages are afforded more privacy than similar messages on the Internet because they are stored for retrieval on AOL's privately owned central computer bank in Virginia. In addition, AOL has a policy not to read or disclose a subscriber's e-mail to anyone (without a court order), thus adding its own contractual privacy protection to any statutory assurances.

While noting that "implicit promises or contractual guarantees of privacy by commercial entities do not guarantee a constitutional expectation of privacy," the court concluded that under the circumstances in this case, the defendant had "a reasonable expectation of privacy, albeit a limited one, in the e-mail messages he sent and received on AOL" (*id.* at p. 417). That expectation of privacy lessened, however, depending on the type of e-mail transmission involved and the intended recipient. "Messages sent to the public at large in the 'chat room' or e-mail that is forwarded from correspondent to correspondent lose any semblance of privacy. Once these transmissions are sent out to more and more subscribers, the subsequent expectation of privacy diminishes incrementally" (*id.* at 419). Despite its holding that a subscriber had some expectation of privacy in AOL e-mail, the court upheld the court-martial of the defendant, determining that the search was not too broad and was reasonable in scope.

In another case involving possession of computer files containing child pornography, an employee of the CIA challenged a search of his computer at his work station on Fourth Amendment grounds. In that instance, his supervisor routinely monitored Internet connections by using a firewall, a device that logs all traffic going outside the network, as well as which computers have accessed the Internet. By checking the firewall log, the supervisor traced a significant number of hits from the employee's computer to pornographic Web sites. From another computer terminal, the supervisor accessed the employee's computer and determined that over one thousand graphic files had been downloaded, some of which contained pornographic images. After obtaining a warrant, copies were made of the employee's hard drive and floppy disks. During the course of his criminal prosecution, the employee-defendant filed a motion to suppress all the evidence obtained, maintaining that the initial search was illegal. The court determined that the defendant had no expectation of privacy in his computer files in light of the CIA policy that permitted audits of the computer network, including file transfers, recording of e-mail messages sent and received, and the URLS of Web sites visited. Moreover, the policy indicated that supervisors were responsible for ensuring appropriate Internet use for all employees under their direction. Consequently, the search was "justified at its inception" because it was the supervisor's duty to monitor Internet activity (United States v. Simons, 1998 U.S. Dist. LEXIS 19646, No. 98-375-A (E.D. Va. Dec. 15, 1998)).

Furthermore, there may be no expectation of privacy when other users have access to the information. In *United States v. Smith*, 978 F.2d 171 (5th Cir. 1992), *cert. denied*, 507 U.S. 999 (1993) the Fifth Circuit refused to find a privacy expectation in conversations taking place on cordless telephones because the conversations may be broadcast to and received by others. The court reasoned that the issue was not whether it was conceivable that someone could eavesdrop on a conversation but if it was reasonable to expect privacy under those conditions. The appellate court went on to observe that changes in the technology could affect the privacy interest: "[a]lthough we express no opinion as to what features or circumstances would be necessary to give rise to a reasonable expectation of privacy, it should be obvious that, as technological advances make cordless communications more private, at some point such communication will be entitled to Fourth Amendment protection" (*id.* at 180).

If, on the other hand, computer communications are analogous to telephone conversations made in conventional secured lines, case law establishes that such conversations are entitled to constitutionally protected privacy (*see, e.g.*, Katz v. United States, 389 U.S. 347 (1967)). Depending on how the courts analogize computer data (i.e., closer to a traditional telephone conversation or one taking place on a cordless telephone), *Smith* may have some predictive value for Fourth Amendment parameters in electronic communications.

For computer systems with security measures that prevent users from accessing each other's data, it can be argued that excluding access by others gives rise to a reasonable expectation of privacy. Software protection that would necessitate circumventing the system in order to read personal data may be sufficient to instill a reasonable inference that other users will not invade an individual's private data.

Nonetheless, a user will probably have no expectation of privacy by the system operator, especially when the operator explicitly states that the user's data are not private (*see* Hernandez, 1988).

Because societal conventions and expectations greatly influence what constitutes an objectively reasonable expectation of privacy, it may be premature to try to ascertain what, if any, aspects of computer communication are deserving of Fourth Amendment protection. If a privacy paradigm is established through use and custom in this relatively new venue, it is probable that, at some time in the future, the courts will recognize some privacy interest in computer information.

State Constitutional Protections

Case law has established that the Fourth Amendment, as incorporated through the Fourteenth Amendment, is applicable to the states (Mapp v. Ohio, 367 U.S. 643, 657 (1961)). As such, it furnishes the threshold requirements for governmental searches and seizures below which no state may fall. In addition, many state constitutions have constitutional provisions resembling the Fourth Amendment. Of those states, at least twelve have provisions that go beyond the purview of the Fourth Amendment and expressly recognize a right to privacy. Moreover, the state constitutions of Florida, Illinois, and Louisiana specifically protect the privacy of personal communications. Thus, state constitutional provisions may provide a higher level of protection for electronic communications than is afforded by the Fourth Amendment.

In addition, some state constitutions have applied the prohibitions on unreasonable searches and seizures to private, as well as public, actors. In the case of *Hill* v. *NCAA*, 865 P.2d 633 (Cal. 1994), for example, the Supreme Court of California interpreted state constitutional privacy protection to apply to private businesses that engaged in information gathering about individuals just as it did to government. Given recent trends that afford increasing importance to privacy protection, it is possible that courts in other states will be persuaded by the rationale in *Hill* to hold private entities to standards comparable to those applicable to the government. In those instances, private institutions will need to be concerned about state constitution protections for students, staff, and faculty, both in the traditional and the electronic format.

Relevant Federal Statutes

Several federal statutes address growing concerns over privacy as technology develops. Several of these laws warrant brief review.

Privacy Act of 1974

The Privacy Act of 1974 (5 U.S.C. § 552(a) (1998)) was passed to promote accountability in the use of computer technology governing personal information systems and government databanks. The Act prohibits, with certain exceptions, government agencies from disclosing any record on any individual for any purpose other than that originally intended without the consent of the individual. The Act also grants to individuals a right of access to their records and the opportunity to amend their records based on a showing of lack of accuracy, relevancy, timeliness, or completion. Personal records include any educational, financial, medical, criminal, or employment records maintained by a federal agency. Violation of an individual's rights under the Act may result in a civil action against the agency for injunctive relief and damages, provided the individual can show harm resulting from the agency's intentional or willful act (5 U.S.C. § 552a(g) (1998)). (For further discussion, *see* Note, *Washington Law Quarterly*, 1976.)

The Privacy Protection Act of 1980

The Privacy Protection Act of 1980 (42 U.S.C § 2000aa(a) (1998)) protects electronic bulletin boards and publicly accessible computer networks from blanket searches and seizures unless probable cause exists that the person possessing such materials has committed or is committing a criminal offense. The Privacy Protection Act limits wholesale seizures of computers where the systems are used for bulletin boards or other general communications unless the operator(s) of the system is directly implicated in illegal activity. Where the system is being used as a conduit for criminal activity only and the operator is not suspected of involvement, the Act requires that no search take place. Instead, law enforcement officials must obtain a subpoena in order to obtain relevant information from the system operator (*see* Fulton, 1994.)

The regulations interpreting the Privacy Protection Act further advise that federal officials may not use search and seizure to obtain documentary material (whether electronically or magnetically recorded) in the hands of disinterested third parties when "a less obtrusive" means of obtaining the material is available (28 C.F.R. §59.1, §59.4(a)(1)(1997)). An exception exists when the integrity of the material (i.e., its availability or usefulness) is somehow jeopardized.

Electronic Communication Privacy Act of 1986

The Electronic Communications Privacy Act (ECPA) (18 U.S.C. §§ 2510 *et seq.*) amended the Federal Wiretap Act of 1968 to include electronic communications.

Title I of the ECPA prohibits government and private citizens from the unauthorized interception of the content of e-mail and computer-to-computer communications. A violation of this section occurs when someone intercepts a private communication while it is in transmission and divulges its contents to a person other than the intended recipient. Title II of the ECPA prohibits the unauthorized access to electronic communications that are stored on a system. In regulating the unauthorized interception of electronic communications, the ECPA focuses on data that are in transit, not with information that is being stored (18 U.S.C. § 2510(17) (1998)). In general, the ECPA makes it illegal to intercept an electronic communication while it is in transmission and to use or disclose the contents of an electronic communication that has been illegally intercepted.

An exception is made for officers, employees, and agents of providers of electronic communications services who may intercept an electronic communication and use or disclose an intercepted communication if the provider is "engaged in an activity which is a necessary incident to the rendition of [its] service or to the protection of [its] property (18 U.S.C. § 2511(2)(a)(I) (1998)). The provider (or its employees) may also disclose and use the intercepted communications under the same circumstances, and may "divulge the contents of any such communication . . . with the lawful consent of the originator or any addressee or intended recipient of such communication . . . [or] to a person employed or authorized, or whose facilities are used, to forward such communication to its destination" (18 U.S.C. § 2511(3)(b)(ii)–(iii) (1998)). In essence, a network provider may intercept almost any communication sent over its network without violating the ECPA.

The ECPA also allows for interception of, or access to, electronic communications when one of the parties to the communication has given prior consent unless such interception is for the purpose of committing a criminal or tortious act. It is unclear if the courts will require that consent be express (i.e., stated in a written policy) or will imply consent from the surrounding circumstances. Also, some state statutes analogous to the ECPA require the consent of both parties before interception is permitted.

Although it is generally illegal to access an electronic communication while it is in storage, the ECPA creates an exception for providers of electronic communications services to access stored communications on their systems. However, a provider of an electronic communications service to *the public* may only divulge the contents of the stored communications with the consent of one of the parties, or if disclosure is necessary to render the service or to protect the rights and property of the provider (18 U.S.C. § 2701(c)(1) (1998)).

Moreover, the ECPA distinguishes between the contents of electronic communication and log files that merely record the fact that an electronic communication was initiated or completed. Accordingly, a service provider may disclose log records to protect itself or a user from fraudulent, unlawful, or abusive use of its system (18 U.S.C. § 2511(2)(h)(ii) (1998)). A provider may similarly disclose a log record, or other information pertaining to a subscriber, to any person other than a government entity without violating the ECPA (18 U.S.C. § 2703(c)(1)(A) (1998)).

One of the few cases construing the provisions of the ECPA is the previously noted Fifth Circuit decision in *Steve Jackson Games, Inc. v. United States Secret Service*, 36 F.3d 457 (5th Cir. 1994). The issue before the court in that case was whether the seizure of a computer used to operate an electronic bulletin board system by the Secret Service violated federal law.

At trial, the evidence established that the seizure of the computer equipment was conducted according to a warrant; at the time of the seizure, there were over 150 unread e-mail messages on the system, which the Secret Service read and then deleted. The district court first found that the Secret Service had violated the Privacy Protection Act by seizing the computer equipment when it had an alternative means of accessing the information stored on the system. Nevertheless, the court refused to find that the Secret Service had intercepted e-mail in violation of title I of the ECPA because its acquisition of the e-mail contents was not contemporaneous with the transmission of those communications (*id.* at 459–60). To access electronic communications during transmission, title I requires law enforcement officials to obtain a court order to minimize interception of communications that should not otherwise be subject to interception. Access to stored communications, under title II of the ECPA, may be obtained under less stringent requirements.

While noting that the Wiretap Act (and thus the ECPA) "was famous (if not infamous) for its lack of clarity" (*id.* at 462), the Fifth Circuit accepted the trial court's interpretation of the relevant portions of the ECPA to mean that the e-mail messages could only be intercepted while the message is in the process of being transmitted. As a result, the decision in *Steve Jackson Games* limits the prohibition on interception to transmissions that are actually being transferred—a process that can usually be accomplished in a matter of seconds. Several other court decisions have similarly concluded that intercepting electronic communications in violation of title I occurs only when the communications are actually in transit, not in electronic storage.

An ECPA case arose recently in the context of higher education. In the case of *Wesley College v. Pitts*, 974 F. Supp. 375 (D.C. Del. 1997), the college and its president sued three individuals formerly employed by the college for alleged ECPA violations associated with the campus computer network. During the course of unrelated litigation with one of the defendants, the president of Wesley College began receiving hard copies of his private e-mail messages in unmarked envelopes at his home. Because the e-mail messages had originally been sent on the college's network system, the plaintiffs—the college and its president—believed that the system had been infiltrated and filed suit against the defendants. One of the defendants, a former faculty member, previously sued Wesley College for breach of contract after he was denied tenure and his teaching contract was not renewed.

On a motion for summary judgment, the defendants argued that the college could not establish an unlawful intercept of the president's e-mails under title I of the ECPA. The defendants had no access to the network either while on campus or after they left. In addition, they did not have the technical capability to access the system from off campus or to use an interception device as required under the statute. The court therefore concluded that it would be "an inferential leap" (*id.* at 390) to affix liability to the defendants under title I, forcing a jury to guess how the e-mails were intercepted. Furthermore, the defendants were also entitled to summary judgment on the title II claim that they had pilfered the president's e-mails from storage because "no rational fact-finder could conclude that [defendants] had the know-how or collaborated with someone who did, to commit such acts" (*id*. at 391). In short, the court refused to find an ECPA violation based solely on innuendo and without concrete evidence of the method used to intercept or access the network communications.

Computer Fraud and Abuse Act of 1986

The Computer Fraud and Abuse Act of 1986 (18 U.S.C. § 1030) criminalizes unauthorized access to computers that are exclusively for the use of a financial institution or the U. S. government. The conduct constituting the offense must directly or indirectly affect the operation of such computers. As such, the Computer Fraud and Abuse Act imposes criminal penalties for hackers who are successful in accessing information on certain government and financial institution computers; the Act does not, however, address the liability of on-line service providers.

Higher education again was the setting for computer activity that resulted in a violation of the Computer Fraud and Abuse Act. In 1991, the Second Circuit considered the matter of *United States v. Morris*, 928 F.2d 504 (2d Cir. 1991), which involved a graduate student in computer science at Cornell University. As a Ph.D. candidate with considerable computer experience and expertise, defendant Morris was provided with a computer account that gave him explicit authorization to use computers at Cornell. The defendant worked on a computer program later known as the INTERNET worm, a program designed to detect inadequacies of security measures on computer networks by exploiting the security defects that were detected. The defendant designed the worm so that once it was inserted at one computer location, it would spread across the entire Internet. According to testimony, the worm did not interfere with normal computer operations nor was it easily found and killed by other programmers.

In November 1988, defendant Morris released the worm from a computer at the Massachusetts Institute of Technology so that no one could trace it to him at Cornell. The worm replicated itself and infected computers on the Internet at a much faster rate than expected, causing many systems to cease functioning. Despite the defendant's belated efforts to try to remedy the problem, computers were infected at numerous locations, including universities, military sites, and medical research facilities. The estimated costs of dealing with the worm at each location ranged from $200 to $53,000.

At trial, the defendant was found guilty of violating the Computer Fraud and Abuse Act. He was sentenced to three years of probation, four hundred hours of community service, and assessed a fine of over $10,000. On appeal, the issue before the Second Circuit was whether the defendant's activities were covered under the statute. Defendant Morris argued that he lacked the requisite intent because he did not intend the damage that resulted from his access. Moreover, he asserted that he was not within the purview of the statute because he had authorized access to the computers at Cornell. The appellate court rejected both of these arguments, determining that Congress did not intend to limit the statute to outsiders to the network system only. "Congress understandably thought that the group most likely to damage federal interest computers would be those who lack authorization to use them. . . . But it surely did not mean to insulate from liability the person authorized to use computers . . . who causes damage to [those computers]" (*id.* at 511).

Damage to computers may also result from "spamming,"—that is, sending bulk e-mails to users of a network. In *America Online, Inc. v. LCGM, Inc.*, 1998 U.S. Dist. LEXIS 20144, No. 98-102-A (E.D. Va., Nov. 10, 1998), a federal district court found that the defendant, a company that operated a commercial pornographic Web site, had accessed AOL's computer network and circumvented AOL's technological filtering controls in order to distribute unsolicited e-mail advertisements about its Web site to AOL's subscribers. The district court held that this activity constituted a violation of a provision of the Computer Fraud and Abuse Act. Thus, spamming constitutes an actionable claim under the federal law (*see also* Hotmail v. Van Money Pie, Inc., 1998 U.S. Dist. LEXIS 10729, No. C98-20064 JW (N.D. Cal. Apr. 16, 1998)).

Economic Espionage Act of 1996

The Economic Espionage Act of 1996 (18 U.S.C. § 1831 (1998)) prohibits the appropriation, concealment, possession, and use of others' trade secrets through illegal means. The Act is applicable to anyone who copies, downloads, or transmits a trade secret, knowing that the offense will benefit a foreign government, instrumentality, or agent. A single offense carries a penalty of $500,000 and fifteen years imprisonment. Although the Act was purportedly designed to prevent international espionage, the consequences of hacking into the wrong computer may be severe. (For further discussion, *see* Bercowitz, 1997.)

Family Educational Rights and Privacy Act

The Family Educational Rights and Privacy Act of 1974 (FERPA), Pub. L. No. 93-380 (codified in scattered sections of 20 U.S.C.), regulates the disclosure of, and access to, education records or personally identifiable information contained in those records without the consent of the student. This law allows students who are enrolled at a postsecondary institution that receives federal funds to review their records on request and to challenge the contents of those records.

The Act also prohibits educational institutions from disclosing the contents of a student's files to third parties except in limited circumstances. For example, an institution may disclose information contained in student records to institution personnel on a need-to-know basis, research organizations, government officials, and persons with an enforcement subpoena (20 U.S.C. § 1232g(b) (1998)).

Recent controversy has arisen over the definition of education records under FERPA that may eventually have an impact on computer logs and records maintained by a college or university. Under FERPA and its accompanying regulations, the term *education records* is broadly defined as all records, files, documents, and other materials that contain information directly related to the student and are maintained by the educational agency or institution (20 U.S.C. § 1232g(a)(4)(A) (1998); *see also* 34 C.F.R. § 99.3 (1997)). The Act does not identify, nor does it limit, education records to any particular type of document, except to specifically exclude records of the institution's law enforcement unit. Thus, the test is whether the record contains information related to the student and whether the record is maintained by the institution. Concurrently, FERPA also prohibits the nonconsensual disclosure of personally identifiable information (i.e., name, parents' names, address, Social Security number, personal characteristics, or other information that would make a student easily identifiable). The statute does list several exceptions to the rule against nondisclosure; for example, an institution may disclose directory information on notification without the consent of the student (34 C.F.R. § 99.3 (1997)).

Even though the U.S. Department of Education maintains a broad interpretation of what constitutes an education record, some courts have been unwilling to grant the same latitude to records receiving FERPA protection. In *State ex rel. The Miami Student v. Miami University*, 680 N.E.2d 956 (Ohio 1997), Miami's student newspaper sought access to all student disciplinary records for a three-year period. The university released the requested records but not until it had deleted all personal information as well as the time, date, and locations of the incidents that gave rise to the disciplinary records. Dissatisfied with the partial disclosure, the student newspaper instituted litigation to obtain the records under the Ohio public records law. The Ohio Supreme Court concluded that the university disciplinary records were not education records within the meaning of FERPA and required the university to comply with the public records request. The Department of Education objected to the ruling and advised the university that it could comply with the court order without violating FERPA only if it redacted all personal information from the records before their release. A federal district court recently ruled that student disciplinary files do qualify as education records under FERPA. Consequently, universities that give explicit information about confidential campus disciplinary proceedings to requests made under state open records laws violate federal privacy law (*see* United States v. Miami University, No. C-2-98-0097 (S.D. Ohio) <chronicle.com/weekly/documents/v46/i30/miami.htm> (Mar. 21, 2000)).

This case has raised questions about what type of documentation maintained by an educational institution will be deemed educational in nature when a request for records is made under a public records statute. The current controversy is limited to disciplinary records, but it may also extend to computer records maintained by the university in its role as a network service provider.

Freedom of Information Act

The Freedom of Information Act (FOIA) (5 U.S.C. §§ 552 *et seq.* (1998)) stipulates that every person has the right to look at any government record unless the disclosure of the record would cause an invasion of privacy. The Act was designed to allow the public to inquire about and monitor government activities. In turn, FOIA placed an affirmative responsibility on the government to make information widely available to those requesting it. In 1994, Congress amended FOIA by enacting the Electronic Freedom of Information Act Amendments of 1996 (EFOIA), Pub. L. No. 104231(codified in scattered sections of 5 U.S.C. § 552 note), to expand the right of individuals, assuring public access to information regardless of the medium in which it was carried; consequently, information cannot be withheld simply because it is in electronic form. Thus, EFOIA gives the public the ability to access government information on the Internet (or other forms of digital media) and to utilize their rights under EFOIA easily and efficiently.

The ability to access public information creates a tension between the public's right to know and an individual's right to privacy. The FOIA does attempt to preserve personal privacy by making certain categories of data not readily available. In addition, the Act requires an agency to delete identifying details that would constitute "a clearly unwarranted invasion of personal privacy" (5 U.S.C. § 552(a)(2)(c) (1998)). In instances where information is redacted from a document or opinion, however, the federal agency must provide justification in writing for the deletion (*see* Freedman, 1987).

There has been a flurry of legislative activity recently involving privacy issues. Since the 106th Congress resumed activity in January 1999, over seventeen new bills concerned with privacy have been introduced with considerable attention devoted particularly to Internet privacy (*See* www.cdt.org/legislation/106th/privacy (visited Feb. 26, 1999). For example, the Consumer Internet Privacy Protection Act of 1999 would regulate the use of personally identifiable information provided by subscribers to interactive computer services (H.R. 313, 106th Cong. (1999)). It is predictable that privacy will continue to be a fertile area for legislation. Commensurately, legislators have also been actively confronting privacy issues on the floor of statehouses.

State Legislation

In addition to federal legislation, many states also have adopted laws to protect an individual's right to privacy in electronic communications. Many of these laws incorporate the provisions of the Electronic Communications Privacy Act of 1986 (ECPA), including the business use and consent exceptions (*see* Hash & Ibrahim, 1996).

In addition to state laws that parallel the ECPA, most states have enacted other privacy laws that may have an impact on electronic communications. In Ohio, for example, a statute (Ohio Rev. Code § 1347 (1998)) governs the operation of personal information systems maintained by state and local agencies (including public educational institutions). The Ohio statute requires the institution to provide notice whenever personal information is placed into a combined or interconnected information system; appoint a compliance officer; collect only information that is necessary for the performance of its duties; maintain only information that is relevant, timely, and complete; and eliminate personal information from the system when it is no longer necessary. Employees of institutions have a right to inspect and contest their records. Violators of the Ohio Privacy Act are subject to civil liability and, in cases of intentional violations, may be charged with a misdemeanor.

State public records laws generally require that public records be available at reasonable times for public review. These laws make all records of public higher education institutions accessible to the public for review. For public institutions faced with a request under these state public records statutes, the possibility exists that the requested information may require disclosure of individual information protected by FERPA. In those instances, compliance with state law may subject the institution to liability under federal law; close attention must be given to potential conflicts that may arise when the institution receives a request for information.

Common Law Privacy Torts

State common law may provide additional avenues for litigation involving alleged privacy invasions of electronic communications. Most states recognize four distinct torts protecting an individual's common law right to privacy: intrusion into seclusion, misappropriation, unreasonable publicity, and false light. Legal causes of action under any of these torts provide recourse against private as well as public entities.

A tort claim of intrusion into seclusion arises when "[o]ne who intentionally intrudes, physically or otherwise upon the solitude or seclusion of another or his private affairs or concerns, is subject to liability to the other for invasion of his privacy, if the intrusion would be highly offensive to a reasonable person" (Restatement (Second) of Torts § 652B (1977)). To prevail on this claim, a person would have to demonstrate that the alleged tortious conduct constituted a substantial intrusion and was highly offensive. The tort of intrusion may exist where an employer maintains a policy that requires employees to submit to urinalysis screening and workplace searches as a condition to retaining employment.

Misappropriation of name or likeness may occur when a person appropriates for his own use or benefit the name or likeness of another (Restatement (Second) of Torts § 652C (1977)). This type of tortious conduct has traditionally been limited to instances involving advertising and other commercial contexts.

Tort law involving public disclosure of private facts subjects a person to liability for invasion of privacy if that person gives publicity to a matter concerning the private life of another (Restatement (Second) of Torts § 652D (1977)) that would be highly offensive to a reasonable person and is not of legitimate concern to the public. These claims may not be based on information that is publicly available or of legitimate public concern. Moreover, First Amendment limitations on claims by public officials and public figures have also been extended to privacy torts, requiring a showing of actual malice (see, e.g., Florida Star v. B.J.F., 491 U.S. 524 (1989)).

The false light tort takes place when "[o]ne who gives publicity to a matter concerning another that places the other before the public in a false light . . . if (a) the false light in which the other is placed would be highly offensive to a reasonable person, and (b) the actor had knowledge of or acted in reckless disregard as to the falsity of the publicized matter and the false light in which the other would be placed" (Restatement (Second) of Torts § 652E (1977)). Courts in some states have refused to recognize the false light tort altogether, finding defamation tort law to provide adequate remedies in this area (see, e.g., Time, Inc. v. Hill, 385 U.S. 374 (1967); for further discussion of privacy torts, see Restatement (Second) of Torts § 652 (1977)).

Given the variety of legal theories that support invasion of privacy, it is not surprising that cases to date have asserted multiple claims for relief. Nevertheless, plaintiffs have only had limited success in prevailing on claims arising out of computer communications.

One such case involved a common law privacy claim against a service provider. In *Stern v. Delphi Internet Services Corp.*, 626 N.Y.S.2d 694 (Sup. Ct. 1995), radio personality Howard Stern sued an Internet service provider for misappropriation of his name and likeness when it published in a newspaper advertisement his photograph with his buttocks exposed. The advertisement was promoting an on-line newsgroup that was devoted to Stern's ill-fated candidacy for governor of New York. The court rejected Stern's claim, holding that the service provider's activity was protected under the First Amendment. The court reasoned that because the defendant used Stern's name to elicit public debate on his candidacy, the subsequent use of his name and likeness in the advertisement was afforded "the same protection as would be afforded a more traditional news disseminator engaged in the dissemination of a newsworthy product. . . . The newsworthy use of a private person's name or photograph does not give rise to a cause of action under [New York law] as long as the use is reasonably related to a matter of public interest" (*id.* at 698–99).

In another case involving common law invasion of privacy, a plaintiff brought a lawsuit against his former employer for wrongful discharge. In *Smyth v. Pillsbury Co.*, 914 F. Supp. 97 (E.D. Pa. 1996), plaintiff Smyth, an at-will employee of defendant Pillsbury, was terminated after he sent e-mails to his supervisor over Pillsbury's internal network in which he threatened to "kill the backstabbing bastards" in sales management and referred to a planned holiday party as the "Jim Jones Koolaid affair." Despite a published policy that all e-mail communications would remain privileged and confidential, the defendant intercepted Smyth's e-mail and then terminated him for transmitting inappropriate and unprofessional comments over the company's e-mail system. The plaintiff subsequently sued the defendant on the intrusion theory of invasion of privacy, arguing that he had relied on the company's assurance that computer communications were confidential and would not be intercepted or used as a basis for discipline or termination (*id.* at 98).

The court dismissed Smyth's complaint for failing to state a cognizable claim and observed that "unlike urinalysis or personal property searches, we do not find a reasonable expectation of privacy in e-mail communications voluntarily made by an employee to his supervisor over the company e-mail system notwithstanding any assurances that such communications would not be intercepted by management. Once plaintiff communicated the alleged unprofessional comments to a second person (his supervisor) over an e-mail system that was apparently utilized by the entire company, any reasonable expectation of privacy was lost" (*id.* at 101). The court then addressed the common law invasion-of-privacy claim, finding that a reasonable person would not consider the interception of the e-mail a substantial or highly offensive invasion of privacy because the plaintiff did not have to disclose personal information about himself or his property. In addition, the court engaged in a balancing test of the company's interests and plaintiff's privacy, determining that "the company's interest in preventing inappropriate and unprofessional comments or even illegal activity over its e-mail system outweighs any privacy interest the employee may have in those comments" (*id.* at 101).

A California court also dismissed employees' invasion-of-privacy claims in *Bourke* v. *Nissan Motor Co.* (Sup. Ct. Cal. 1991, unreported). In that case, plaintiffs were former employees who were hired to set up and operate an e-mail system between defendant Nissan and its dealers. The employees were warned by their supervisor to discontinue using the e-mail system for inappropriate jokes and language. The employees complained about the e-mail monitoring and were eventually fired. The defendant successfully asserted that the employees had no reasonable expectation of privacy in their messages because they had signed a computer registration policy that restricted the use of company computers for business purposes only. (For additional discussion of the topic of monitoring employee e-mail, *see* Hash & Ibrahim, 1996.)

Implications for Higher Education

In its new role as a service provider of a campus computer network, the institution must be aware of the legal and policy ramifications of the privacy rights of its users, whether students or employees. The university should also be aware of its legal avenues of recourse against third parties or users who abuse or circumvent security measures on a university-owned system.

Hacking Incidents

As computer use escalates, so do incidents of computer hacking on campus networks. Hacking incidents are not limited to outsiders; colleges and universities have found that students are often involved in security incidents. In one incident, a student at the University of Colorado stole passwords and passed them to an Israeli hacker via an Internet chat room. The student had obtained the passwords using a packet sniffer, and the hacker later tried installing similar programs in an attempt to gain greater access to the network. (A packet sniffer is a program that secretly monitors information as it flows across a network and can record anything typed by a user, including passwords, e-mail messages, and credit card numbers.)

Although most network administrators agree that attacks by skilled hackers are rare, they are nevertheless on the rise. In the recent well-publicized hacker attacks on major Web sites (CNN, eBay, and Amazon.com), computers on at least three university campuses were involved. There is no indication that the hacking was initiated from campus networks, but there is speculation that campus-based computers may have been used because university systems are not well secured, allowing hackers to deposit programs on the university computers that could later be utilized in the attack (*see* Kiernan, 2000).

In yet another incident, a half dozen computers on Virginia Tech's network were attacked by hackers who deposited secret payloads, or small packages of instructions, that were intended for further attack on the university network. If the payloads had gone undetected by network administrators, the second attack could have crippled the university system (*see* Olsen, 2000).

Incidents involving novice hacking are increasing as well, largely as a result of the availability of hacking programs on the Internet. As these amateur hackers test their limits on the network, they can inadvertently interrupt service or even cause major damage.

Institutions are exploring ways to better secure their networks from hacker attacks. At the same time, administrators must be aware that security measures may impinge on the privacy rights accorded users. In reviewing the constitutional, statutory, and case law relating to privacy interests, several general principles emerge to guide administrators in their approach to promoting a secure campus network. For purposes of clarity, they have been framed in terms of user privacy interests (including students and faculty) and university interests.

Providing for User Privacy Interests

The seminal question raised in any privacy litigation, whether based on constitutional or common law, focuses on the issue of the individual's reasonable expectation of privacy. As a general rule, an expectation of privacy will be found to exist when the individual has both a subjective and objective expectation that his or her electronic communications are private. If there is no reasonable expectation of privacy, there is no Fourth Amendment protection; no warrant or probable cause is required. Thus, consideration of a reasonable expectation of privacy will involve the following factors:

who owns the system, who has access to the system, whether the system is password protected; and what policies and practices apply to the system (*see* McDonald, 1999).

Some institutions have dealt with this issue by advising its users that they have no expectation of privacy in information stored on or transmitted over the university's system. The underlying theory is that there can be no subjective belief that one's e-mail is private if the user is told up front that the institution is monitoring the computer network.

Yet higher education institutions must be cautious in undertaking any monitoring of the system other than for administrative purposes. As discussed extensively in previous chapters, the more control the university exerts in the communication process, the more likely the institution will incur liability for abuses of expression and copyright. In addition, Fourth Amendment standards indicate that there should be individualized suspicion of misconduct before a search is permitted, thus precluding random searches and widespread monitoring. This requirement also is supported by the mandates of the ECPA (and the parallel state laws) that generally prohibit the interception, access, or disclosure of personal electronic communications. The ECPA does permit the university service provider to intercept communications in transit or access communications stored on its system for business purposes only. Although the scope of the ECPA is not entirely clear, it appears that an educational institution may not routinely monitor all electronic communications it carries without justification or consent.

Privacy tort law has not yet afforded much relief for users in the electronic environment. Courts have been willing to recognize a limited expectation of privacy in e-mail but have generally found in favor of the institution when balancing individual privacy interests against those of the institution in maintaining appropriate and business-related communications on its system. The university is in a somewhat different position than an ordinary employer given the various constituencies (students, staff, and faculty) as well as its educational mission. With First Amendment issues and privacy interests involved, courts may perceive the institution's right to monitor differently from the right of a business operation to do the same.

At a minimum, however, the institution must implement procedures and technological methods to prevent dissemination of student records that are deemed educational records within the meaning of FERPA. At the present time, the secretary of the Department of Education has advised that student e-mail is considered an education record (*see* Campbell, 1999). Although no additional guidance has been forthcoming, such a determination may raise the level of encryption or other security devices required to protect e-mail from being accessed by outsiders or persons within the institution who lack a need to know.

Protections guaranteed by the Family Educational Rights and Privacy Act (FERPA) may become an issue in situations in which the e-mail records of one student are accessed legally but include e-mails from another student entitled to protection of his or her educational records. In reference to a question posed earlier, a university confronted with a request for a student's e-mail records by the FBI should respond only to a subpoena or court order and should have administrative procedures in place to redact personal information from e-mail generated to or by other students at the university before complying with the subpoena.

Institutions must be equally careful when putting sensitive student records on-line so they may be viewed by the student. Some colleges employ a Web-based system designed to give students easier access to their transcripts, bills, and other information. Colleges that open student records to parents electronically have to be concerned with student privacy issues as well as FERPA violations. To that end, the institution should require the informed consent of the student and password encryption before posting information about students on-line (*see* McDonald, 1999).

Private institutions should not necessarily be solaced by the fact that they are not subject to the requirements of the Fourth Amendment when it comes to privacy issues on their computer networks. Even though it is clear that federal constitutional restrictions do not apply to private searches, at least one court has held that once law enforcement officials are notified of the existence of illegal material (e.g., child pornography) on a computer hard drive, any further investigation of the hard drive by private parties must comply with Fourth Amendment requirements (*see, e.g.*, United States v. Barth, 26 F. Supp. 2d 929 (W.D. Tex. 1998)). Moreover, state constitutional provisions may constrain searches in a private institution. Absent constitutional prohibitions, there are still ample laws to provide a remedy for privacy violations, including the ECPA, its state law equivalents, and state tort laws.

Most of the legal issues concerning student privacy interests can be addressed by formulating computer use policies that are carefully drafted to provide adequate notification to users of the institution's policies and procedures. Not only will such policies prevent misunderstandings between users and network administrators, but they may assist courts in ascertaining the extent of privacy rights in the unfortunate event of litigation. Courts are generally willing to recognize (and possibly defer to) contractual provisions respecting privacy. Thus, an acceptable use policy should, at a minimum, establish the user's expectation of privacy (ranging on a continuum from total privacy to no privacy) and obtain the consent of the user to administrative searches. As privacy law emerges in this area, it may be advisable to revisit these policies; nevertheless, until the law changes, these are critical threshold requirements.

Protecting University Interests

In addition to protecting the rights of its users, the institution must protect its rights as the owner-operator of the network. It is undisputed that the university would have a privacy interest in its computer system; hence, searches by law enforcement officials require a warrant.

Court decisions to date indicate that a student's e-mail correspondence on a university network may be accessed by law enforcement officers and is discoverable in litigation. In one instance, a New York man was convicted of sexually assaulting a Columbia University student that he met on-line. The victim maintained an Internet account on the computer system at Columbia, whereas the defendant had an AOL account. The defendant asserted that the sexual activity was consensual and requested copies of the victim's e-mail messages stored on the university network. Despite several attempts to block production of the e-mail records, the court ultimately decided that a redacted version of the e-mail messages was discoverable (New York v. Jovanic, No. 10938/96 (N.Y. Sup. Ct., 1997)).

Given the increasing frequency of e-mail correspondence, it is likely that such correspondence will be subject to subpoenas and court orders. Colleges and universities should have in place an established administrative procedure to follow when such requests are made and consult with counsel if there is any doubt about compliance with a judicial order.

Because of the system configuration, computer records produced in compliance with such a warrant may require the network administrator to access communications not required in the warrant; where communications are inadvertently accessed as a part of system function, the contents should be kept confidential. A court order may also require interception of communications while they are in transit on the system. It is clear from the cases to date that the requirements under title I of the ECPA are more stringent; therefore, the institution officials should comply only with the specific requirements of the warrant for the specified length of time.

If the institution has cause to believe that a particular user is abusing the system, administrative searches (i.e., purging expired mail or performing system backup) should be conducted by the least intrusive means available. For example, the system administrator investigating the content of a user's hard drive might perform a limited search by scanning the disk for key words (e.g., sexual terms) instead of viewing the entire content of a user's e-mail; moreover, this should be done only if it is suspected that the particular user is guilty of infractions. If the system administrator intends to copy files from a user's computer, the administrator may want to temporarily lock out the user while the files are copied and then obtain the user's consent or a warrant before viewing the files in their entirety.

The scope of a law enforcement search of university computer records is further limited by the requirements of the Privacy Protection Act. Under that Act, law enforcement agencies cannot seize computer equipment when there is an alternative method available to obtain university computer records.

As noted earlier, technological encryption is a rapidly changing arena that may have implications for institutions of higher education. For instance, the use of digital certificates is being explored by several institutions. Digital certificates are small bits of code that are used to prove the identity of users in computer interactions. These digital certificates essentially use two cryptographic keys— one public and one private—that authenticate the identity of the computer contacting the server. Although this form of technological security has the potential to make on-line activity secure from hacking attempts, the cost of implementing digital certificates can be limiting (see Olsen, 1999). With respect to the security employed by the institution on its own system, better encryption may result in a system that is harder to penetrate. However, better encryption may simultaneously increase the user's expectation of privacy in his or her communication on the network.

Criminal Activity

Although most of this discussion has been devoted to the institution's protection of its users and its network, there should be no doubt that users of the system may be held liable for on-line abuses or hacking and that such activities may be criminal in nature. Both the Computer Fraud and Abuse Act, the Electronic Communications

Privacy Act (ECPA), and the Electronic Espionage Act make hacking a federal crime. Computer users, whether on or off campus, may also be prosecuted under state laws with ECPA-like provisions. Hence, the disgruntled professor who hacks into the personnel files of his former university may be facing criminal penalties if the requisite statutory elements can be proven.

Recommendations

1. **Require compliance with applicable laws and policies.**

   Every policy should require users to comply with all applicable law, both state, federal, and local. As evidenced in previous chapters, these can be quite extensive. Federal laws include the Copyright Act, the Electronic Communications Privacy Act, and the Computer Fraud and Abuse Act, among others. Relevant state laws, both statutory (i.e., state public records laws, state ECPA laws, antipornography and stalking laws) and common law (i.e., defamation, privacy) also apply. University rules and policies (e.g., student conduct code, sexual harassment policy) as well as applicable software contracts and licenses are also binding on users and should be incorporated by reference into the policy.

   The policy should advise that each user is responsible for ascertaining and complying with all of the foregoing; however, it is *not* recommended that an explanation of all the laws, contracts, rules, or policies be included in the policy. Such an undertaking would not only be burdensome but could later be construed as imposing liability on the institution if a student claimed he had relied on such information when he or she was actually violating a law. As noted earlier, courts would likely construe information contained in the policy as part of the contract between the institution and the user and may find that the university has assumed the responsibility for disseminating all legal information if it attempts to do so in part.

2. **Prohibit unauthorized use of computer accounts.**

Users need to be advised that they must use computing resources only to the extent authorized; in other words, their ability to access material or accounts other than their own does not imply that they have the authority to do so. Unauthorized use should include accessing or using another's computer account, supplying false information in order to gain such access, or sharing an account with another user. Sharing of files or a printer does not justify sharing an individual's computer account.

If the campus network system is protected by password use, the user should also be advised that he or she is responsible for taking precautions to protect individual passwords. Because the institution cannot absolutely guarantee secure communications, a disclaimer may be included, essentially stating that the institution cannot protect those users who engage in electronic communications or disclose personal information on the Internet.

3. **Advise users of system operation.**

In addition, users need to be aware that the use of campus computing networks is not completely private. The normal operation and maintenance of a system requires backup and caching of data, logging activity, and other legitimate reasons for monitoring. Users should be made aware that the institution occasionally monitors activity related to the rendition of the network service; furthermore, the policy should articulate the conditions under which a user's account may be subject to monitoring. These might include circumstances under which the integrity of the system is jeopardized (e.g., an individual account has excessive activity) or when the system administrator has reasonable cause to believe that the user is violating the acceptable use policy (e.g., on notification of alleged copyright infringement or defamation). Users should also be aware that their communications posted to newsgroups are accessible to the network administrator as well as to most Internet users.

4. **Establish expectation of privacy.**

Institutional service providers are in the unique position of being able to establish in advance the expectation of privacy for their users in their computer policy, thereby limiting their own exposure to liability for privacy violations. Prior to policy implementation, institutions must determine what level of privacy they can and should afford their users. If total privacy is permitted, institutions must be prepared to take the necessary steps to ensure security of communications. At the other end of the continuum, some institutions have chosen to provide no privacy at all, subjecting all electronic communications to possible scrutiny by the institution. Another option is to provide partial privacy by providing a password-protected system, yet reserving the right for the institution to monitor or access private communications in certain circumstances. If partial privacy is to be afforded, the policy should set forth the criteria that must exist for the university to access the contents of computer accounts and the procedure to be followed.

Once the institution determines its position on electronic privacy, it should be stated in the acceptable use policy. Use of the system should be conditioned on the user's consent, which can be obtained by having the user sign a copy of the policy or having the user consent on-line each time he or she accesses the network, or both. After consent has been obtained to the terms and conditions of the policy, the expectation of privacy set forth in the policy has effectively been created; both the user and the institution will be bound by the policy. In addition, securing consent to access user communications under specified circumstances also avoids potential liability of the institutional service provider under the ECPA's consent exception.

Conclusion

Heightened concern about the potential loss of privacy in the electronic venue has propelled legislators to enact a myriad of laws designed to ensure the privacy of electronic communications. When coupled with the existing framework of constitutional and common law, privacy law has become a mosaic of complex, overlapping principles that attempt to balance individual privacy interests with public interests in and to information. Given the emergent nature of privacy law at this time, it is difficult to predict whether traditional privacy guarantees will operate in an electronic environment.

For institutional service providers, prudence dictates that the interests of the greater university community take precedence over individual privacy interests. Once computer policies are articulated, they should be consistently and stringently followed.

4

Fairness and On-Line Dispute Resolution

The very nature of cyberspace defies constraints of time and space. It is undisputed that, once connected to the Internet, a network's system will generally be available to anyone with a computer and a modem anywhere in the world. A provider of Internet access will have minimal control over those who access its system; similarly, a user will have little control over who views his or her communication. Several recent cases have been filed against American universities in British courts for alleged defamatory remarks made by a student on a university network. These cases raise a perplexing question: What court has legal jurisdiction to hear the case?

In addition to jurisdictional concern in litigation, other fairness issues relate to constitutional and contractual guarantees of due process for users of the institution's systems. There are those who argue that computer data have become property in the information age (*see, e.g.*, Chaplowski, 1991). If courts adopt this view, there may be constitutional protections involved for public institutions. Even more important, perhaps, is the need for institutions to provide due process in their procedures that comport with notions of fairness for individual users, yet benefits the university community as a whole. For instance, how should a university approach a student accused of e-mail harassment? Should the university's handling of the matter change when that student resides in another state and is enrolled solely in courses offered via the Web?

Higher education institutions are potentially affected by procedural matters such as due process and jurisdiction as the service providers for their respective campus computer networks. These issues will inevitably have an impact on the institution's practices and policies for network use.

Due Process

As discussed in previous chapters, campus computer networks can be abused in a number of respects, ranging from copyright infringement to transmission of child pornography. Some of these abuses have the potential to result in civil litigation or criminal prosecution. Not surprisingly, most abuses constitute an infraction of university computer policies.

Policies for acceptable use of computer networks on campuses may provide separate disciplinary measures for abuses of the computer network, or the policy may specify that misconduct on the network will be handled through normal university disciplinary policies applicable to the user. One aspect of due process requires that violations of rules or regulations be clearly understood by those affected; consequently, it is imperative that acceptable use policies be drafted with specificity, both as to the nature of the violation and the resulting consequences. Policies must not be vague but must be written in terms understandable to the university population.

Those charged with formulating the policy should contemplate what disciplinary sanctions can be invoked in the event of computer misuse. If suspension or dismissal can result from a violation, then the policy must comply with minimum due process requirements. The following discussion briefly reviews those requirements in educational institutions.

Due Process in Educational Settings

As noted previously, adjudication of a claim alleging a due process violation involves a judicial determination of whether the person claiming the violation had a property or liberty interest at stake;

whether governmental action infringed on such an interest; and whether adequate due process procedures were followed. Although property rights are created by state law (*see, e.g.*, Board of Regents v. Roth, 408 U.S. 564 (1972)), courts have traditionally held that under state law the establishment of colleges and universities open to the public creates an entitlement for enrolled students (*see, e.g.*, Siblerud v. Colorado State Bd. of Agriculture, 896 F. Supp. 1506 (D. Colo. 1995)). Courts have therefore generally assumed that a student's continued enrollment in a public educational institution constitutes a property right for purposes of due process analysis (*see*, for example, Marin v. University of Puerto Rico, 377 F. Supp. 613, 622 (D.P.R. 1974), in which the court found a property interest in continued enrollment at a public institution).

A student's liberty interests may also be implicated in disciplinary action on campus. Liberty interests are involved when a public college or university takes an action that as a result of the notoriety or stigma attached to it would harm someone's reputation, honor, integrity, or ability to find employment (*see, e.g.*, Goss v. Lopez, 419 U.S. 565 (1975); Board of Regents of State Colleges v. Roth, 408 U.S. 564 (1972)). Consequently, courts have held that the suspension or expulsion of a student may seriously harm the student's reputation, potentially preclude the student from completing his or her education at another institution, and eventually affect the student's ability to engage in the student's occupation of choice (*see, e.g.*, University of Tex. Med. Sch. v. Than, 901 S.W.2d 926 (Tex. 1995)).

Extracurricular Activities

Due process is generally not a concern when a student is denied participation in extracurricular activities as a result of alleged misconduct. The vast majority of courts that have considered participation in athletics, for example, have held that termination does not require hearings or other procedural protections (*see, e.g.*, Pegram v. Nelson, 469 F. Supp. 1134 (M.D.N.C. 1979) (exclusion from all extracurricular activities for the remainder of the academic year did not implicate a property interest); Palmer v. Merluzzi, 689 F. Supp. 400 (D.N.J. 1988) (sixty-day suspension from all extracurricular activities did not implicate a property interest)). No property interests attach to extracurricular activities as they are considered a privilege rather than a right in the educational process. Accordingly, computer network use that is defined as a privilege would be analogous to an extracurricular activity.

Procedural Requirements

The Fifth Circuit in Dixon v. Alabama Board of Education, 294 F.2d 150 (5th Cir. 1961), cert. denied, 368 U.S. 930 (1961), considered the case of several students who had been expelled from Alabama State College for engaging in civil rights activities. On appeal, the court made it clear that the Due Process Clause of the Fourteenth Amendment "requires notice and some opportunity for hearing before students at a tax-supported college are expelled for misconduct" (id. at 158). The court then established the standards by which the public institution's procedures should be measured: "The notice should contain a statement of the specific charges and grounds which, if proven, would justify expulsion. . . . The nature of the hearing should vary depending upon the circumstances of the particular case. The case before us requires something more than an informal interview with an administrative authority of the college. This is not to imply that a full-dress judicial hearing, with the right to cross-examine witnesses, is required" (id. at 158).

Thus, without expressly deciding the issue, the court in Dixon assumed a property interest of the plaintiff students and the requirement of due process procedures. In 1975, the Supreme Court spoke to the issue of due process in educational settings. In Goss v. Lopez, 419 U.S. 565 (1975), the Court considered the level of due process required prior to the suspension of a high school student. It concluded that a secondary school student facing a suspension of less than ten days was entitled to due process by receiving "some kind of notice and . . . some kind of hearing" (id. at 579). The Court in Goss was not willing to afford students the right to a full-blown adversary hearing (i.e., cross-examination, written transcripts, representation by counsel); only minimal requirements were necessary to comply with the due process clause. "[T]he student [must] be given oral or written notice of the charges against him and, if he denies them, an explanation of the evidence that the authorities have against him and an opportunity to present his side of the story" (*id.* at 581).

Although the focus for due process in educational settings remains on the notice and opportunity-for-hearing requirements of *Dixon* and *Goss*, there is also latitude in tailoring proceedings to specific circumstances. In deriving guidance from existing case law, it is evident that notice to the student should include both the conduct with which the student is charged and the rule or policy that has allegedly been violated. The notice should include sufficient detail to enable the student to present a defense at the hearing. Advance notice of the charges is clearly required; however, courts have found acceptable as little as two days' notice. (For further analysis of notice requirements, *see* Kaplin & Lee, 1997.)

Minimum hearing requirements oblige institutions to give students the opportunity to speak and explain their version of the alleged misconduct. Hearings may be open to the public or closed at the discretion of the institution or, if given the choice, the student. Failure to provide the right to cross-examination, to counsel, to transcripts, and to appeal does not violate due process in most circumstances. Where university policy gives students the right to appeal, however, stated appeal procedures must be followed, but some courts have viewed these as enhancements to due process procedures (Henson v. Honor Comm. of the Univ. of Va., 719 F.2d 69 (4th Cir. 1983)).

Furthermore, the hearing should take place before the suspension or expulsion goes into effect unless the student presents a danger if allowed to remain on campus (Goss v. Lopez, 419 U.S. 565, 583 (1975)). In rendering a decision, the hearing officer must not consider evidence that has not been made known to the student on the theory that the student would not have had the opportunity to shed a different light on or explain the undisclosed evidence (*see*, *e.g.*, University of Tex. Med. Sch. v. Than, 901 S.W.2d 926 (Tex. 1995)).

An institution is not precluded from simultaneously pursuing disciplinary action when the conduct is criminal. The courts have held that noncriminal sanctions imposed by a college or university do not constitute punishment; accordingly, the student has not been exposed to double jeopardy within the meaning of the law. One court observed that concurrently pursuing disciplinary action is obligatory on the institution to provide redress for victims and prevent students from manipulating the institutional system for their benefit. "Educational institutions have both a need and a right to formulate their own standards and enforce them; such enforcement is only coincidentally related to criminal charges and the defense against them. To hold otherwise would . . . lead logically to the conclusion that civil remedies must wait for determination until related criminal charges are disposed. . . ." (Nzuve v. Castleton State College, 335 A.2d 321 (Vt. 1975)).

Due process requirements will increase, however, when the conduct leading to a disciplinary hearing is also the subject of proceedings in criminal court. In those instances, the student is entitled to additional constitutional protections (i.e., right to counsel) to guard against self-incrimination in the parallel criminal action (*see*, *e.g.*, Gabilowitz v. Newman, 582 F.2d 100, 104 (1st Cir. 1978) (requiring institution to allow student to have an attorney present to advise him at the disciplinary hearing); *see also* Donohue v. Baker, 976 F. Supp. 136 (N.D.N.Y. 1997)).

State Administrative Procedures Acts

For states with administrative procedure codes in place, the due process procedures contained in the codes are binding on public institutions and will be applicable to disciplinary hearings for students or employees (i.e., faculty or staff) of the college or university. In states that have alternative informal procedures, it may be necessary (and prudent) to obtain a written election of the less rigid format from those involved to avoid subsequent due process claims.

Private Institutions

Because the due process requirements of the Fourteenth Amendment and state administrative procedure codes apply to tax-supported public institutions only, private colleges and universities are, as a general rule, free to offer whatever level of due process they choose. On rare occasions, courts have found private institutions to have engaged in state action, mandating that they provide the same constitutional protections as public entities (see, e.g., Buckton v. NCAA, 366 F. Supp. 1152 (D. Mass. 1973); VanLoock v. Curran, 489 So. 2d 525 (Ala. 1986). For additional discussion of state action concepts as applied to private institutions, see American Law Reports Federal, 1978.) More often, however, courts limit their inquiries to a determination that the process afforded to a student was consistent with the policies of the private institution.

Essentially, courts will require private institutions to follow their own rules. The decision of a private institution to discipline its students, therefore, must be predicated on procedures that are fair and reasonable, lend themselves to a reasonable determination, and are substantially observed (see, e.g., Tedeschi v. Wagner College, 427 N.Y.S.2d 760 (Ct. App. 1980)). This requirement to follow stated procedures may be expressly stated in the laws of the state in which the institution is located, or the courts may consider the relationship between private colleges and their students to be contractual in nature. Statements in student handbooks and policies are used to determine the terms of the contract (see, e.g., Corso v. Creighton Univ., 731 F.2d 529 (8th Cir. 1984)).

Application to Campus Networks

If the sanction imposed as a result of the disciplinary process is to deny access to the computer network, either temporarily or permanently, it is unlikely that a court would consider such action a deprivation of a property interest under current case law. In all probability, the court would determine that the computer network was extracurricular in nature and not an entitlement of the student. This analysis might change, for example, if the student were engaged in on-line course instruction or if an instructor required the student to use the Internet for a course and no alternative sources of information were available. In those instances, or even when the student has paid a computer fee in addition to tuition, a court might find that the institution had afforded the student a right of access, and due process protections may attach.

Furthermore, there is some speculation that the legal definition of a property interest may change in the future to reflect the growing importance of information in today's society(see Chaplowski, 1991). If, in fact, the courts would equate information with property, then denial of access to one's information by a public institution may necessitate due process protections.

The lack of a property interest notwithstanding, there is a possibility that the court could also find a liberty interest at stake. This might be problematic in the event that a student was denied access to the Internet via the campus network and yet was unable to gain access through a private contract with another service provider (e.g., because of the configuration of the campus system). In theory, this could preclude an individual from acquiring useful knowledge, thereby implicating a liberty interest. Moreover, any disciplinary action for accessing sexually explicit material (i.e., Internet pornography) could also be stigmatizing if the allegations were made public.

Until courts engage in a redefinition of property and liberty interests, however, the legal paradigm suggests that no measures need be taken prior to denial of access. Acceptable use policies may specify that the institution may temporarily suspend or block access to a user's account, before the initiation or completion of other disciplinary measures, when it reasonably appears necessary to do so to protect the integrity of the system or to insulate the university from liability.

Once it is determined that a violation has occurred, procedures set out in the applicable policies (i.e., acceptable use policy or student conduct code) should be strictly adhered to; if a computer violation constitutes an infraction under student codes, those codes should be amended accordingly.

Specificity in explaining the charges is of particular importance in the context of misconduct on a campus network, especially in light of the fact that some prohibited activity may be performed by a novice user. In addition, it is likely that those involved in the judicial affairs process on a campus have more experience with misconduct in the real world than they do with virtual misconduct. From the university's perspective, it may be helpful to have technical assistance in evaluating alleged violations and the exact technical methods used. In an environment of disparate levels of computer expertise, it is critical that those prosecuting the violation and the alleged violator are on a level playing field to ensure due process.

If the suspected violation carries potential criminal liability, university policy should state that the matter will be referred to the appropriate law enforcement officials. Under these circumstances, the institution should implement additional due process protections in pursuing disciplinary action, minimally allowing the attendance of counsel at the hearing. In states with administrative procedure laws, public institutions should ascertain whether the due process afforded under its policies exceeds the threshold requirements of state law; once those minimal requirements are met, the additional protections given in policies are discretionary with the institution. When alternative levels of due process are offered, the student or employee should be permitted to elect one only if university policy requirements will thereby be met.

Faculty Privileges

Misconduct on campus computer networks is not limited to students alone; there are numerous examples of employee (i.e., faculty and staff) misuse as well. Denial of network access to faculty members for suspected misuse may have more serious ramifications because it could be deemed an infringement on the faculty member's academic freedom. Suspension of a faculty member's access should not take place before the alleged violation is investigated and the proper disciplinary channels followed. In adjudicating the matter, adequate due process must be afforded, particularly if the infraction may result in termination of employment.

Courts have repeatedly held that a tenured faculty member has a property interest in continued employment. Nontenured faculty also have a property interest in employment for the duration of the employment contract, although nonrenewal of employment may be achieved without a hearing. Universities that undertake to remove a faculty member without some form of due process are definitely at risk for litigation. Even suspension of computer privileges may subject the institution to a claim that a faculty member's academic freedom has been violated and thus requires due process.

Given the changing level of technology, policies may need to be reconsidered and reformulated at more frequent intervals; moreover, experience with computer infractions may lead to policy changes. Nevertheless, it is incumbent on public and private institutions to follow existing policy until a new policy is formally in place and the university community has been informed.

Due process in the context of campus computer networks does not warrant a paradigm change; it is only the nature of the misconduct that has changed. Institutions, both public and private, may wish to afford students and faculty the same considerations for infractions on computer networks as they do for any other type of misconduct on campus. However, the more complicated the procedures, the more cumbersome they become to implement.

On-Line Dispute Resolution

Increased levels of communication on computer networks heighten the chance for conflict between users; at the same time, however, the network also presents opportunities to design on-line forums to resolve such conflicts. Moreover, resolving controversies on-line circumvents jurisdictional and choice-of-law problems that occur in real-world courts. The merits of alternative dispute resolution have generated much discussion and several projects have been piloted. (For an excellent article about on-line dispute resolution, *see* Katsch, 1996.)

Two methods of dispute resolution have been explored: *arbitration*, in which a controversy is actually resolved by a group of arbitrators who are well acquainted with Internet technology, customs and traditions; and *mediation*, in which communication between the parties to a dispute and a mediator are structured to facilitate agreement between the parties. The Virtual Magistrate Project (VMP), (<vmag.law.vill.edu:8080>), is an example of on-line arbitration developed in 1995 by the Villanova Center for Information Law and Policy. The primary purpose of the VMP is to resolve disputes between system operators arising out of messages or postings that may put the system operator at risk (i.e., alleged copyright infringement, defamatory or obscene messages). For example, a complainant might assert that a second party had posted a defamatory message on a system under the control of another service provider and demand that the message be deleted. Under the auspices of the VMP, the parties would submit their version of the facts through e-mail messages to a magistrate, who would render a decision within two to three days. A dispute may be considered by a single *virtual magistrate* (a person who resolves disputes in an on-line forum) or a panel of three arbitrators selected from a pool.

Because the VMP occurs solely in cyberspace, there are no concerns with jurisdictional matters as in a court. The magistrate's jurisdiction extends only to the parties that have agreed to the arbitration; hence, third parties cannot be bound by the decision of the magistrate. According to VMP rules, a magistrate may not consider applicable contracts and general substantive law only, but may consider rules of etiquette as well. While the VMP is relatively new, it is hoped that arbitral opinions will eventually form a body of customary law on which subsequent decisions may rely. (For additional information on the VMP, *see* Post, 1999; Gellman, 1999.)

Another on-line dispute resolution service is the Online Ombuds Office, (<www.ombuds.org>), sponsored by the University of Massachusetts. Unlike the VMP, however, this service provides mediation for disputes rather than arbitration. Like traditional ombuds services, the role of the on-line ombudsperson is to listen to the parties, provide information, frame issues, develop options, make referrals, and generally assist parties in helping themselves. The Online Ombuds Office pairs an ombudsperson with someone who has technical expertise and experience with the Internet to assist in putting on-line disputes in context. In addition, mediation takes place not only via e-mail but in chat rooms to allow for real-time communication among participants to the mediation process (Katsch, 968).

In sum, the technology that gives rise to cyberdisputes is being used to resolve those disputes as well. Higher education institutions are pioneering efforts to create on-line forums for resolving controversies that arise on the Internet in an effort to keep regulation of the Internet out of the hands of the courts. Although any efforts to relieve the overcrowded dockets of our courts are welcome, the on-line forum method of dispute resolution is not a panacea for every conflict arising in the electronic arena. Arbitration and mediation, whether on-line or off-line, require the willingness of all parties to submit to third-party intervention. In an increasingly diverse population of users in cyberspace, the requisite level of cooperation might not be forthcoming in all situations, especially where disparate levels of Internet expertise exist.

Jurisdictional Issues in Cyberspace

Institutions of higher education and their constituents are entitled to due process in disputes arising in cyberspace. A critical component of due process is the judicial forum selected to resolve such disputes. Traditional concepts of jurisdiction (i.e., where a lawsuit can be initiated) are primarily focused on geographical boundaries.

Linking to global computer networks has removed, or at least shifted, constraints of time, place, and distance; hence, there has been some consternation over how to handle cyberdisputes in real-world courts. One commentator believes that traditional notions of jurisdiction might be outdated in a world that is now divided into networks, domains, and hosts rather than into nations, states, and provinces (*see* Faucher, 1993). Another commentator contends that jurisdictional concepts are flexible enough to accommodate this shift (*see* Weiner, 1995.) Put simply, the crux of the debate is the extent to which computer network users and providers should be subject to lawsuits brought in courts all over the country, or even the world, for their on-line activities.

While the legitimacy of the correspondence between legal and physical borders for on-line controversies continues to be argued, courts are beginning to confront this dilemma. One case that pinpoints the dilemma involved a California couple who distributed pornography over the Internet. They were prosecuted in Tennessee, judged by Tennessee standards, and sent to jail for several years, even though the computer files never left California and would not have been considered pornographic under the standards of that state (United States v. Thomas, 74 F.2d 701 (6th Cir. 1996), discussed in detail in Chapter Three).

When disputes in cyberspace are taken into the courts, jurisdictional and choice-of-law issues are the first requiring resolution; if the litigation has not been brought in the proper forum, any finding on the merits of the controversy will likely be overturned on appeal. An overview of the legal framework for determining jurisdictional matters follows.

Basic Legal Framework

To entertain a lawsuit, a court must first have jurisdiction over the subject matter; then it must ensure that it also has jurisdiction over the parties. Generally, courts have personal jurisdiction over defendants who consent to be sued in the state, are physically present in the state, reside in the state, and commit torts or conduct business in the state. Most challenges to personal jurisdiction arise with respect to the last category: whether the defendant conducted business in the state. So-called long arm statutes, which allow local forums to obtain jurisdiction over nonresident defendants when a lawsuit affects local plaintiffs, set forth the circumstances under which a court may exercise jurisdiction over an out-of-state defendant. However, the Due Process Clause of the Fourteenth Amendment has been interpreted as limiting the ability of a forum state to exercise personal jurisdiction.

In *Pennoyer v. Neff*, 95 U.S. 714, 722 (1877), the Supreme Court held that the courts of a state cannot subject persons outside the state to its decisions without due process of the law. Courts since *Pennoyer* must now establish the basis for asserting jurisdiction over a nonresident defendant. The defendant's contacts with the state must be substantial enough to ensure fundamental fairness under the Due Process Clause. In other words, a defendant cannot constitutionally be sued in a state unless those contacts were sufficient to warn the defendant that "he should reasonably anticipate being haled into court there" (World Wide Volkswagen Corp. v. Woodson, 444 U.S. 286, 297 (1980)). In short, a defendant will be required to bear the cost and inconvenience of defending a lawsuit in another state only if the requirements of a state's long arm statute are met *and* the statute is consistent with constitutional standards of fairness.

Jurisdiction on Computer Networks

Against this backdrop of principles governing in personam jurisdiction, courts have recently been confronted with adjudicating issues of personal jurisdiction on computer networks. *CompuServe v. Patterson*, 89 F.3d 1257 (6th Cir. 1996), *reh'g en banc denied*, 1996 U.S. App. LEXIS 24796 (September 19, 1996), was a Sixth Circuit decision that involved a dispute between a commercial service provider and one of its customers. In that case, CompuServe, an

Ohio-based provider of computer information services, filed a lawsuit against one of its subscribers who resided in Texas.

Despite the fact that the defendant had never been to Ohio and had sold his software to only twelve Ohio residents for a total of $650, the Sixth Circuit found that the defendant had, when subscribing to CompuServe, entered into a contract that expressly stated it would be governed by and construed in light of Ohio law. In addition, defendant Patterson initiated the events that led to the filing of the Ohio lawsuit by making demands of CompuServe via electronic and regular mail messages. The court concluded that the test for personal jurisdiction had been met: "[Defendant] purposefully availed himself of the privilege of doing business in Ohio. He knowingly reached out to CompuServe's Ohio home, and he benefitted from CompuServe's handling of his software and the fees that it generated" (*id.* at 1266–67). The court did distinguish the situation in *Patterson* from an ordinary suit for collection of subscriber fees: "Merely entering into a contract with CompuServe would not, without more, establish . . . minimum contacts with Ohio" (*id.* at 1265).

Other judicial decisions have also found personal jurisdiction solely on the basis of a minimal number of electronic communications. In one instance, a California court found business transactions conducted solely over the Internet and telephone lines constituted sufficient contacts despite the fact that they were exclusively electronic (Hall v. LaRonde, 66 Cal. Rptr. 2d 399, 402 (Ct. App. 1997)).

By contrast, other courts have been unwilling to find jurisdiction on almost identical facts. In *Bensusan Restaurant Corp. v. King*, 937 F. Supp. 295 (S.D.N.Y. 1996) *aff'd*, 126 F.3d 25 (2d Cir. 1997), the defendant, who owned a jazz club in Missouri called The Blue Note, set up a Web site promoting his establishment. Potential patrons could find the club's telephone number and order tickets on its Web site. The plaintiff was a proprietor who owned a club of the same name in New York City and had obtained a federally registered trademark for The Blue Note. He sued the Missouri defendant for trademark infringement in a New York district court. The sole jurisdictional allegation in the complaint was that defendant King had established a Web site in Missouri that was accessible to New York residents. The court held that fact to be insufficient to support New York jurisdiction over the defendant: "Creating a site, like placing a product into the stream of commerce, may be felt nation-wide—or even worldwide—but without more, it is not an act purposefully directed toward the forum state" (*id.* at 301).

As more cases involving the issue of jurisdiction are being decided, a clearer set of principles is being delineated. The determinative factor appears to be the commercial nature of the activity conducted on the Internet. One court observed that there is a positive correlation between the willingness of a court to exercise personal jurisdiction and the commercial activity of an out-of-state defendant:

> [O]ur review of the available cases and materials reveals that the likelihood that personal jurisdiction can be constitutionally exercised is directly proportionate to the nature and quality of commercial activity that an entity conducts over the Internet. This sliding scale is consistent with well-developed personal jurisdiction principles. At one end of the spectrum are situations where a defendant clearly does business over the Internet. If the defendant enters into contracts with residents of a foreign jurisdiction that involve the knowing and repeated transmission of computer files over the Internet, personal jurisdiction is proper. At the opposite end are situations where a defendant has simply posted information on an Internet Web site which is accessible to users in foreign jurisdictions. A passive Web site that does little more than make information available to those who are interested in it is not grounds for the exercise of personal jurisdiction. The middle ground is occupied by interactive Web sites where a user can exchange information with the host computer. In these cases the exercise of jurisdiction

is determined by examining the level of interactivity and commercial nature of the exchange of information that occurs on the Web site.

(*Zippo Mfg. Co. v. Zippo Dot Com, Inc.*, 952 F. Supp. 1119, 1123–24 (W.D. Pa. 1997) (footnotes and citations omitted).)

Choice of Law

Even when a forum state determines that it has jurisdiction over a defendant in a case arising in cyberspace, it still faces the issue of what body of substantive law is applicable to the case. Courts will first look for the existence of an agreement between the parties to the dispute as to which law is applicable (e.g., a contract that expressly states it is governed by the laws of a specified state). In the absence of any such agreement or regulation (i.e., in the case of tortious conduct), courts have to resolve this matter by applying choice-of-law principles.

Traditional choice-of-law theory has focused on two theories: the older theory is known as *lex loci delicti*, or "the place of the wrong;" a second theory adopts a most significant relationship approach to resolving conflicts of laws. The *lex loci delicti* approach examines where the last event necessary to make an actor liable took place and thus determines the applicable law. With respect to tortious conduct, the *lex loci delicti* is the state in which the injury or damage occurred. This theory is problematic for disputes arising in cyberspace, largely because it is increasingly difficult to identify the location of a transmission; under this analysis, the place of the wrong could be either the place where an offending transmission was initiated or where it was received. Because of the difficulty in making this determination, the potential arises for a court to favor the laws of its forum state, especially if there is no clear indication of where the controversy actually arose (*see, Keeton v. Hustler Magazine, e.g.*, 465U.S. 770 (1984)), applying New Hampshire law to libel in a nationwide publication.

A later approach to determining what law to apply employs the most significant relationship approach to the choice of law. It permits the court to engage in a balancing of interests between respective states and parties in determining the location of the most significant relationship (*Restatement (Second) of Conflict of Laws* §145(2) (1971)). Although certainly a more flexible concept than the first, the most significant relationship approach is still geographically fixed.

Determining the appropriate law to apply in cases involving diverse parties and jurisdictions is often difficult in real life controversies; for cases arising in an electronic venue, the analysis is even more complex because traditional legal rules do not translate easily to a borderless setting. If, as noted previously, the judiciary is confronted with this dilemma, it may be inclined to favor its own laws in resolving these types of disputes. That proclivity, as well as the broadening concepts of personal jurisdiction for Internet cases, may encourage forum shopping, permitting prospective plaintiffs to look for a court in which their case would receive the most favorable treatment under the law.

International Issues

In the international arena, laws in other countries can present opportunities for litigation that would not be recognized in the United States. For example, in the United Kingdom, libel is a strict liability tort, requiring no proof of intent or damage. In Canada, communicating hate speech is a crime; moreover, the Canadian definition of obscenity is much broader than that in the United States. As a result, what may constitute a tort or a crime in one country may be dramatically different in another. (For further discussion, *see* Branscomb, 1993.)

Electronic communications that enjoy First Amendment protection in this country may become criminal when they cross international lines. For example, a computer bulletin board operated by a group in the United States known as the Aryans Nations Net promoted white supremacy and maintained a list of targets for extermination (*see* Branscomb, 1993). These messages could be accessed in Canada, where they were illegal. However, only with the cooperation of U.S. authorities could the Canadian authorities obtain extradition orders or jurisdiction. A pervasive feature of modern extradition principles is double criminality, which requires that the charged offense be criminal in both the jurisdiction requesting extradition and the jurisdiction from which it is requested.

Because global networks and transmissions are a fairly recent phenomenon, issues of jurisdiction and choice of law have been infrequently litigated. However, there are instances in which actions have been brought in foreign courts against United States citizens for radio transmissions that violated foreign laws. In *Pindling* v. *National Broadcasting Corp.*, 49 O.R. 2d 58 (1984), an Ontario court exercised jurisdiction over American broadcasters for allegedly defamatory statements about the then prime minister of the Bahamas. The only connection to the judicial forum was that the broadcast was seen and heard in Canada. The court specifically noted the benefit to the plaintiff in using the Canadian forum: "the real advantage to the plaintiff in bringing the action in Ontario is that it is not necessary to establish 'actual malice' " (*id.* at 65).

Notwithstanding the ramifications of being sued in foreign countries, there are preliminary indications that American courts may not be willing to enforce foreign judgments obtained by forum-shopping plaintiffs. In *Bachchan* v. *India Abroad Publications, Inc.*, 585 N.Y.S.2d 661 (Sup. Ct. 1992), an Indian national had obtained a libel judgment in an English court against a New York news service operator. The subject of the libel suit was a wire service story transmitted only to India. The plaintiff then sought to have the judgment enforced in a New York court. The court refused, recognizing that English law did not provide First Amendment protections nor did it require the plaintiff to prove fault on the part of the defendant, as he would have had to do under American jurisprudence. The court concluded that enforcement of the judgment would be unconstitutional: "The protection of free speech and the press . . . would be seriously jeopardized by the entry of foreign libel judgments granted pursuant to standards deemed appropriate in England but considered antithetical to the protections afforded . . . by the United States Constitution" (*id.* at 665).

Similarly, another U.S. district court refused to recognize a libel judgment obtained in an English court based on public policy grounds, concluding that the "recognition and enforcement of a foreign judgment, based on libel standards that are repugnant to the public policies of . . . Maryland and the United States, would deprive the plaintiff of his First and Fourteenth Amendment rights" (Matusevitch v. Telnikoff, 877 F. Supp. 1, 2 (1995)).

In a recent case, a British scientist agreed to settle a defamation lawsuit filed in an English court against Cornell University for insulting comments about him that were posted to the Internet by a student using the Cornell network. The scientist's claim against the university was based on the fact that he asked Cornell officials to remove the offensive comments and they declined, citing First Amendment considerations. Had the litigation been filed in a U.S. court, Cornell would have been immune under section 230 of the Communications Decency Act. There is no similar exception under British law. Therefore, Cornell would either have to appear and defend the action in the United Kingdom, or contest the foreign judgment when it was brought to the United States for execution. In the same case, the British court awarded a judgment of more than $80,000 against the Cornell student who made the comments (*see* Kaplan, 1999).

Ramifications for College Service Providers

The foregoing case raises the question of whether institutions of higher education as network providers will be subject to jurisdiction anywhere in the world. Arguably, university and college service providers should not have jurisdictional concerns; they typically operate from a single system in a single state; they do not have subscribers from different states, as in the case of a commercial service provider. The possibility of being subject to international jurisdiction raises substantial and troubling issues, essentially requiring the institution to control the millions of messages that flow through its systems and to be an arbiter of foreign law.

Potential jurisdictional issues are also possible when a higher education institution offers asynchronous distance learning over its network. The college or university that chooses to offer coursework via the Internet to residents of other states may simultaneously be subjecting itself to personal jurisdiction in that state. Likewise, a college or university that contracts with or enters into partnerships with on-line course providers needs to define jurisdiction and choice of law when drafting its agreements with those third parties. Under such circumstances, the courts may find that the institution has purposely availed itself of the privilege of doing business in another state by accepting students and directing the dissemination of course materials to students in that state. Providing such an educational service for nonresident students in exchange for the payment of tuition is clearly contractual, much the same as it is with students who are physically present for classes on campus. If earlier court analysis is followed, the contractual arrangement, together with the repeated transmission of communications via the Internet, will be sufficient contact to justify personal jurisdiction.

Because of the possibility that litigation may arise from contracts formed, performed, or breached in cyberspace, institutions may want to resolve jurisdictional uncertainties in advance by including a forum selection clause in the materials that form the contract. A forum selection clause specifies which state's (or nation's) law applies to the contract. By adding a choice-of-law clause, institutions will ensure that the litigation forum will uphold the favored body of substantive law in adjudicating the case before it (see Smiddy, 1986; Zaphiriou, 1988).

Generally, courts are inclined to give weight to forum selection and choice-of-law clauses; the assumption is that they reflect the expectations of the parties to the contract. Law and forum selection in contracts will generally be honored so long as the choice is reasonable. To be deemed reasonable, there must be "connecting factors" to the forum selected, and the choice must not be oppressive to a party as the result of a gross inequality of bargaining power (*see, e.g.,* Carnival Cruise Lines v. Shute, 499 U.S. 585 (1991)). Even though courts may find selection-of-law clauses in adhesion contracts more suspect, they have nevertheless upheld forum selection clauses even when bargaining parity is lacking. Given this predisposition, it is likely that a forum selection clause between a large institution and an individual student will be enforceable, even if the agreement is a standard form contract or simply a visual notice on the computer screen.

Many universities already incorporate their rules of use before allowing a student or faculty network access. Under these circumstances, incorporating a forum selection and choice-of-law clause should not present any difficulty (*see* Burnstein, 1996).

In light of this possibility, institutions should consider including a provision in their registration materials for nonresident distance learning students specifically stating that in the event of controversy any suit must be brought in the home state of the institution. The student's signature on the registration materials would indicate his or her assent to this provision and would likely result in a dismissal of an action instituted in another state.

On-line application or registration to the institution by students outside the state may also increase the chances of personal jurisdiction in another state. Although strictly passive sites are probably excluded, an interactive Web site that requires an exchange of information may subject an institution to jurisdiction, depending on the level of interactivity and the commercial nature of the activity. Although application and registration to an educational institution are not commercial in the traditional sense, it cannot be disputed that an institution is marketing its educational services via its Web site. As noted above, the inclusion of a short jurisdictional statement in registration materials would effectively preclude a disgruntled applicant or student from filing a nuisance suit in another state.

This is not to imply that the institution can not prevail in the absence of a forum and law selection clause. In the absence of a forum selection clause or other effective choice of the parties, the courts would probably employ the significant relation test by considering the place of contracting, the place of negotiation, the place of performance, the location of the subject matter of the contract, and the domicile or place of business of the parties. In addition, it is possible that the court would decline jurisdiction on the grounds of *forum non conveniens*. Under this doctrine, the court has discretionary power to decline jurisdiction when convenience of the parties and ends of justice would be better served were the case to be heard in a different jurisdiction. Despite the fact that cyberspace confounds notions of place and location, it is still likely that the institution would prevail under this analysis. Because the provision of educational services is the subject matter of the contract and those services are performed in the institution's home state (or in the case of distance education is initiated there), a court would be hard pressed to find a more significant relationship with a state whose only connection to the controversy is the student's home residence.

Although defending a lawsuit in a neighboring state may not be particularly onerous, being forced to litigate in other countries would be expensive and more hazardous if the laws differ substantially from our own. As more institutions offer distance education on a global basis, the possibility of litigation abroad increases commensurately. However, concerns of institutions without significant assets abroad may be assuaged by the fact that United States courts have not been willing to enforce foreign judgments against United States citizens when the judgment is obtained under different legal standards. Institutions with tangible or intangible property located in other countries may nevertheless have those assets subject to attachment if a foreign judgment is levied on them.

On a positive note, an educational institution should find it easier to pursue its legal remedies against those who violate the legal rights of the institution, or those it represents. For example, under current jurisdictional analysis, actions for copyright or trademark infringement of on-line materials could be brought in a federal court sitting in the institution's home state. Similarly, tort actions for defamation or invasion of privacy occurring on-line could be maintained in the forum state against nonresident third parties, provided the appropriate jurisdictional criteria were satisfied.

In summary, the institution's role in providing the campus computer network also requires it to provide access to other networks that cross state and national borders. Consequently, colleges and universities that have heretofore never been concerned with jurisdictional and choice-of-law issues must now be cognizant of them. These issues are further complicated by the inability to apply traditional concepts to an electronic venue that has no geographical boundaries, leaving the courts to formulate new rules on a case-by-case basis. Until such time as clear principles emerge with respect to jurisdictional issues on the Internet, institutions should proceed cautiously when transmitting coursework or otherwise interacting with nonresidents via the Internet and should obtain consent to home state jurisdiction when possible.

Recommendations

The following recommendations may help avoid fairness issues that may arise in disputes arising out of the use of campus computer networks.

1. Define access to the campus network as a privilege.

Computer network access provided by the institution should be defined as a privilege rather than a right. Many institutions already incorporate this language; the purpose is to prevent users from demanding access as a form of entitlement, requiring instead that their on-line conduct earns them the right to continued use of the campus network. This written expression acts as a notification to the user that computer use can be kept only through appropriate usage. Not only does such a statement aid in understanding, but it reduces the necessity of formal due process before a user can be removed from the system. It should be noted, however, that the court is not precluded from finding a property interest because of such a statement, especially if academic freedom interests are involved in the suspension of a faculty member's access.

2. **Consider limiting sanctions for misconduct.**

The institution may want to consider limiting discipline for infractions of computer policies to loss of computer privileges; suspension or expulsion should only be considered in the event of serious or repeated problems and only after due process has been afforded to the same extent it would be provided for an alleged violation on the physical campus. Although temporary suspension of privileges is permissible for students because computer usage is an extracurricular activity, it is ill advised to target a faculty member's account because of concerns over academic freedom. For that reason, due process should be provided before suspension of the faculty's computer privileges.

3. **Incorporate forum selection and choice-of-law clauses.**

As outlined in this chapter, forum selection and choice-of-law clauses are increasingly important in computer use policies, particularly where transmissions are being sent across state lines. Although the contractual obligations in the acceptable use policy extend only to the user and the institution, a greater number of out-of-state students may be using the computer networks in distance learning situations. It is also prudent for on-line admissions applications and registration to carry similar provisions to avoid the institution being haled into court in another jurisdiction. The selection clauses can be handled in one or two sentences and are simply added protection for the institution in the event it is sued in another state.

4. **Consider on-line dispute resolution.**

A final suggestion for policy promulgation is that the use of on-line dispute resolution should be considered as an alternative to the existing student judicial systems on college campuses. Although these on-line methods of alternative dispute resolution are only in their infancy, they do provide a forum for systematic review of disputes by individuals who are well versed in the technology and its legal parameters. Furthermore, they are operated by other institutions of higher education and are sensitive to the academic culture as well. For colleges or universities with student judicial systems that are not designed to deal with cyberspace matters, on-line dispute resolution may present an attractive alternative. Moreover, it presents an existing neutral forum for disputes arising between faculty members and administration or between faculty members themselves. Should this prove to be a viable alternative, the policy should reflect that the institution and users agree to initially submit disputes to mediation or arbitration with a specified dispute resolution service before pursuing any legal remedies available to the parties.

Epilogue

The legal issues raised in this book—potential intellectual property disputes, free speech concerns, and privacy—have been identified by noted scholars as having critical legal ramifications for higher education (Kaplin and Lee, 1997). These legal issues have created the need to develop policies as campuses join the emerging cyberspace community.

In the early 1990s, very few institutions had published policies covering use of an institution's computing facilities; most administrators were only vaguely aware of the existence of the Internet. Today, every person in the university community understands the need to be linked to the Internet for research and communication. Many institutions are still in the process of developing computer or acceptable use policies for the first time; still others have policies in place that may need to be revised as new questions arise with changes in technology or the law.

As institutions struggle to draft policies to handle theoretical conflicts, actual controversies illustrate the complexities associated with the implementation of these policies in the university community. At one institution, a dispute arose between a faculty member and campus administrators who forbade the faculty member to use campus computers to send e-mail messages to a long list of addresses, including listservs. The administration banned the professor from using campus computer facilities after the institution was threatened with litigation arising out of the professor's allegedly defamatory messages made on-line. The professor filed a grievance under the faculty union contract. At the same time, however, he posted the university's disciplinary directive on-line, bringing a deluge of protests from academics and listserv participants around the world (Monaghan, 1999).

Faculty have not been the only ones to challenge computer use policies; a student at Southern Utah University actually forced a controversy by asking other students to complain about the pornographic and white supremacist Web sites that she was visiting, resulting in her expulsion from campus computer labs. Both students and faculty complained about the new policy, arguing that it was overly broad. Since the incident, the university committee responsible for creating the policy has met to review and revise the current version (Monaghan, 1999).

Similar challenges to university policies that attempt to regulate speech and conduct on campus networks may be anticipated, especially in the higher education environment, which is particularly sensitive to issues of intellectual freedom. Although it is not possible to foresee every eventuality in drafting computer use policies, legal parameters exist that can be followed to ameliorate controversy, while at the same time contributing to the positive attributes of network use.

The final point of inquiry should examine whether the benefits associated with providing campus computer networks outweigh the risk of legal liability associated with it. At this juncture, the response is in the affirmative, particularly in light of the recent legislation that immunizes the institution for most copyright and tort abuses perpetrated by their users. If this predisposition in favor of service providers who merely act as carriers or conduits of computer transmissions is indicative of a trend, institutional service providers can rest easier. This does not imply, however, that institutions can become lax in policy formulation and implementation. Good policies are characterized by simplicity rather than legalese and should be revisited frequently to reflect changes in the law. The Checklist and Guidelines that follow will help formulate such policies and practices. In order for legal risks to be effectively managed, network administrators should remain vigilant for abuses occurring on the networks and take steps to eliminate them. When fiscally feasible, technological developments that improve on problematic areas such as privacy should be considered.

The technological revolution that has taken place on college and university campuses in less than a decade is unprecedented. Institutions have embraced the era of computers by incorporating them into every aspect of academia. In this rapidly changing environment, further change in technology and the law is inevitable. As both service providers and educational institutions, colleges and universities are uniquely positioned to help shape the emerging legal and regulatory landscape of computer networks. Participation in the ongoing debate may influence the future of the electronic environment, thereby protecting institutional investment and ensuring the appropriate utilization of this new educational resource.

Resources

Checklist for Developing Computer Use Policy

- Determine if computer policy will be permissive or restrictive in scope with regard to computer network use in light of the underlying philosophy and mission of the institution.

- Create a process of policy development that allows input by the university community as a whole.

- Allow review by administrators, students, and faculty to determine if the policy is sufficiently clear, succinct, and understandable.

- Have counsel and committee review to ascertain if the policy is potentially:

    vague (i.e., can its prohibitions be comprehended by those affected by the policy?)

    overbroad (i.e., does it sweep protected expression into a proscribable category?)

    underinclusive (i.e., does it proscribe certain kinds of expression but not others?)

- Include a provision in the policy that requires every user to comply with all applicable laws, whether federal, state, or local.

- Include a provision in the policy that requires compliance with all university rules and policies (e.g., student conduct code, sexual harassment policy) as well as applicable software contracts and licenses.

- Determine procedures to assist users in obtaining relevant legal information. Some suggestions include the following:

  provide network users with the telephone number or e-mail address of a resource person on campus who can address their questions

  provide users with the address of Web sites that contain information on copyright or other laws related to electronic conduct

  have competent counsel prepare a separate document with an overview of the relevant copyright, libel, privacy, obscenity, and hacking laws. Update and circulate this document regularly and include a highly visible disclaimer that it is not intended to be comprehensive or to provide legal advice.

- Include a provision in the policy that defines use of university-owned computers and the network as a privilege rather than a right.

- Include a provision that users have authority to access assigned accounts only; users' ability to access material or accounts other than their own does not imply that they have the authority to do so.

- Prohibit commercial activity by users, or any activity for personal financial or other types of gain that are not related to educational purposes or advancement.

- Include language that requires users to limit their use to what would be considered reasonable by others in the university community. Alternatively, incorporate an "honor" provision, asking users to recognize the finite capacity of the institution's computing facilities and to refrain from consuming unreasonable amounts of those resources.

- Include a statement that users do not have permission to use institutional trademarks or logos on their personal transmissions or Web pages, or engage in conduct in which the user might be perceived as a representative of the institution.

- Specify that the policy will be enforced and that a permanent loss of computer privileges or other specified repercussions may result from internal adjudication of the matter.

- Provide users with information about the requirement of federal copyright laws and include a statement promoting compliance with those laws.

- Include an express provision setting forth the unequivocal right of the institution to terminate access in instances where users have engaged in copyright infringement on more than one occasion.

- Determine if the institution will formulate its own rules for assessing fair use. Fair use guidelines should be disseminated in the university and be available on-line.

- Provide for a copyright resource office that can answer questions and assist in obtaining copyright permission where fair use is contraindicated, or even questionable.

- Determine a model for ownership of digitized intellectual property and incorporate appropriate provisions in copyright policies as well as collective bargaining agreements if applicable.

- Require separate individualized contracts for the development of multimedia or on-line course materials.

- Avoid any language that could be construed as regulating the content of on-line speech.

- Establish as a matter of policy what level of privacy will be afforded on the campus network. Incorporate language that sets what level of privacy users can expect.

- Require all users to consent, in writing, to the provisions of the computer policy before they are given access to the network.

- Include forum selection and choice-of-law clauses in the policy and any on-line documents (i.e., applications, registration materials).

- Set forth in detail the due process procedures that will be followed in the event of alleged violations of the policy. In cases of student violations, follow the existing student conduct code or limit procedures to notice and opportunity to be heard.

- Consider the viability of campus or on-line dispute resolution; if adopted, require arbitration or mediation as prerequisite to pursuing any other legal remedies in contract language.

Guidelines for Network System Administrators

1. NAs are responsible for educating users about the operation of the system and the computer use policy, and should collaborate with student affairs professionals in programming activities.

2. NAs should keep apprised of changes in technology and applicable laws governing computer networks and inform the appropriate groups or administrators of changes that may affect the operation of the system.

3. Accessing and monitoring user files by NAs should be limited to administrative necessity (i.e., situations in which files must be deleted or archived to free up space).

4. NAs and their employees must maintain the confidentiality of files read inadvertently.

5. NAs should appoint an on-line agent for infringement notification, notify the U.S. Copyright Office of the identity of the agent, and otherwise comply with that DMCA provisions. Procedures should be implemented and followed in the event notification is received by the agent of an alleged infringement occurring on the campus network.

6. Once a NA has been notified of infringing or defamatory material being transmitted or stored on the computer network, appropriate steps should be taken to delete the offending files.

7. In the event the NA suspects criminal activity on the network, the NA should notify appropriate law enforcement agencies.

8. In emergency situations in which there is an immediate threat to the operation or security of the network, NAs may take any action necessary to preserve the integrity of the system.

9. When a NA receives a subpoena or court order requesting computer files or information about a user, the NA should consult with counsel for the university in providing only those records requested. In cases where student computer records are involved, identifying information about other student users should be redacted from the records.

Glossary of Terms

Answer—the pleading filed by the defendant in response to the plaintiff's complaint.

Appellant—the party who requests that a higher court review the actions of a lower court.

Appellee—the party against whom an appeal is taken (usually, but not always, the winner in the lower court).

Bill—a legislative proposal introduced in the legislature that has not been enacted into law.

Bulletin board system—two-way computer communication services usually managed by hobbyists or commercial computer networks.

Caching—storing partial or complete duplicates of materials from frequently accessed sites to avoid repeatedly requesting copies from the original server.

Case law—law created by reported judicial decisions.

Cause of action—a claim in law and fact sufficient to bring the case to court; the grounds for a lawsuit.

Certiorari—a writ issued by a superior court requiring a lower court to produce the records of a particular case. A writ of certiorari is a discretionary device used by the Supreme Court to select the cases it wishes to hear.

Chilling effect—to intimidate so that a person refrains from speaking.

Common law—largely customary unwritten law; serves as the foundation of the American legal system.

Complaint—the initial pleading that includes a statement regarding the court's jurisdiction, a statement of the claim upon which relief is sought, and the relief requested.

Cyberspace—a term coined by William Gibson in *Neuromancer* (1984), referring to the digitized arena of electrons connecting one computer to another.

Damages—monetary compensation awarded by a court for an injury caused by the act of another.

Defamation—the offense of injuring a person's character, fame, or reputation by false and malicious statements; the term includes both libel (written) and slander (oral).

De minimis—from the phrase *de minimis non curat lex*, which means that the law does not care for, or take notice of, very small or trifling matters.

Digitize—to put data into digital notation (by numerical expression) for use in a computer.

Domain name—the name an individual or entity uses to identify its Web site.

Downloading—the transfer of information from a bulletin board or the Internet to a personal computer.

Due process of law—a term found in the Fifth and Fourteenth Amendments of the Constitution and also in constitutions of various states. Although subject to various interpretation, it is concerned with the guarantee of a person's rights in courts of justice.

Freedom of expression—the liberty to express opinions and facts uncontrolled by any censorship or restrictions of government.

Hacker—a person who views and uses computers as objects for exploration and exploitation.

Hypertext markup language (HTML)—formatting technique on the Web in which certain text is highlighted in order to link it with another document.

Injunction—a judge's order that a person or entity do or refrain from doing a certain act.

Internet service provider (ISP)—any individual or entity—commercial, nonprofit, or educational—that provides access to the Internet for a specified group of users.

Judicial review—the review of legislation or other governmental action by a court to determine whether it is constitutional.

Judicial supremacy—the Supreme Court's right to review the constitutionality of federal and state court decisions.

Jurisdiction—the power of a court to make legally binding decisions over certain persons or property or a geographical area.

Liability—the condition of being responsible for damages resulting from an injurious act.

Obscenity—conduct tending to corrupt the public morals by its indecency or lewdness.

Opinion—an expression of the reasons why a certain decision or judgment was reached in a case. A majority opinion is usually written by one judge and represents the principles of law to which a majority of the judges subscribe. A separate opinion may be written by one or more judges which concurs (agrees) or dissents (disagrees) from the majority opinion. A plurality opinion is agreed to by less than a majority of the judges as to the reasoning but agreed to as to the result. A per curiam opinion is an opinion by the court that expresses a decision without identifying the author.

Overbreadth doctrine—serves to invalidate legislation so sweeping that, along with its allowable proscriptions, it also restricts constitutionally protected rights of free speech, press, or assembly.

Pornography—that which is obscene or licentious. Material is pornographic or obscene if the average person, applying contemporary community standards, would find that the material, taken as a whole, appeals to a prurient interest, if it depicts in a patently offensive way sexual conduct, and if the work taken as a whole lacks serious artistic, political, or scientific value.

Regulations—rules or orders issued by various government agencies to serve as guidelines for the law.

Remand—the action of a higher court in sending a case back to a lower court for further proceedings.

Spamming—using a computer network to send a single message to thousands of recipients.

Stare decisis—the doctrine of American law that states that when a court has formulated a principle of law as applicable to a given set of facts, it will follow that principle and apply it in future cases where the facts are substantially the same.

Strict liability—liability without fault.

Tort—a private or civil wrong or injury.

Uniform resource locator (URL)—string of letters and numbers that identifies a Web location to users.

Uploading—transfer of information from a user's computer to a computer network, usually via a bulletin board.

Vagueness doctrine—basis for striking down a law or regulation that does not fairly inform a person or give sufficient warning of what conduct is unlawful.

Vacate—to render an act void, such as to vacate an entry of record or a judgment.

Vicarious liability—the imposition of liability on one person for the actionable conduct of another, based solely on the relationship between the two persons.

Web site—a number of interconnected pages, each of which consists of a separate computer display of textual or graphic information or both.

(*Note:* Definitions of legal terms were taken from *Black's Law Dictionary*, 6th ed., 1990 and Jacobstein, J. M., Mersky, R., and Dunn, D. J. *Fundamentals of Legal Research*, 6th ed., 1994.)

References

"Annotation: Action of Private Institutions of Higher Education as Constituting State Action or Action Under Color of State Law for Purposes of the Fourteenth Amendment and 42 U. S. C. S. § 1983." *American Law Reports Federal*, 1978, 37, 601.

Bercowitz, L. G. "Economic Espionage Act of 1996: An Experiment in Unintended Consequences?" *Colorado Lawyer*, Dec. 1997, 26 (1247), 47–50.

Branscomb, A. W. "Jurisdictional Quandaries for Global Networks." in *Global Networks: Computers and International Communication*. Cambridge, Mass.: MIT Press, 1993, 83–104.

Burgoyne, R. "The Copyright Remedy Clarification Act of 1990: State Educational Institutions Now Face Significant Monetary Exposure for Copyright Infringement." *Journal of College and University Law*, 1992, 18, 367–379.

Burk, D. L. "Ownership of Electronic Course Materials in Higher Education." *Cause/Effect*, Fall 1997, 20, 13–18.

Burke, A. "Man Pleads No Contest, Fined in Cyberporn; Sun Valley Man Possessed Child Pornography Downloaded from the Internet." *Los Angeles Daily News*, June 30, 1995, 7.

Burnstein, M. "Notes: Conflicts on the Net: Choice of Law in Transnational Cyberspace." *Vanderbilt Journal of Transnational Law*, 1996, 29, 75–116.

Campbell, E. E-Mail correspondence. Family Policy Compliance Office, U.S. Dept. of Education, May 25, 1999.

Chaplowski, F. S. "Note: The Constitutional Protection of Information Privacy." *Boston University Law Review*, Jan. 1991, 71, 133–160.

DuBoff, L. D. "An Academic's Copyright: Publish and Perish." *Journal of the Copyright Society*, 1985, 32, 17–38.

Dueker, K. S. "Trademark Lost in Cyberspace: Trademark Protection for Internet Addresses." *Harvard Journal of Law and Technology*, 1996, 9, 483–512.

Durfee, D. "Man Pleads No Contest in Stalking Case." *Detroit News*, Jan. 25, 1996, D3.

Faucher, J. D. "Comment, Let the Chips Fall Where They May: Choice of Law in Computer Bulletin Board Defamation Cases." *University of California at Davis Law Review*, Summer 1993, 26, 1045–1078.

Field, T. G., Jr. "Copyright on the Internet." <www.fplc.edu/tfield/copyNet.htm>, Mar. 20, 2000.

Foster, A. "Plans for New Domain Suffixes Have Colleges Girding for Fresh Trademark Fights" *Chronicle of Higher Education*, <chronicle.com/free/2000/07/2000070701t.htm>, July 7, 2000.

Franke, A. H. and Michelson, M. "Pressures Today on Faculty Academic Freedom in American Higher Education." Paper presented at the 20th annual national conference of Stetson University College of Law on Law and Higher Education, Feb.11–13, 1999.

Freedman, W. *The Right of Privacy in the Computer Age*. New York: Quorum Books, 1987.

Fulton, A. M. "Cyberspace and the Internet: Who Will Be the Privacy Police?" *CommLaw Conspectus*, 1994, 63–70.

Gellman, R. "A Brief History of the Virtual Magistrate Project: The Early Months." <www.law.vill.edu/ncair/disres/Gellman.HTM>, Apr. 1, 1999.

Grossman, M. and Hift, A. K. "Anticybersquatting Act Leaves Many Questions Unanswered." *Texas Lawyer*, 2000, 62.

Hash, P. E. and Ibrahim, C. M. "E-Mail, Electronic Monitoring and Employee Privacy." *South Texas Law Review*, June 1996, 37, 893–910.

Hernandez, R. T. "ECPA and Online Computer Privacy." *Federal Communications Law Journal*, 1988, 41, 17–41.

Johnson, D. R. and Marks, K. A. "Mapping Electronic Data Communications onto Existing Legal Metaphors: Should We Let Our Conscience (and Our Contracts) Be Our Guide?" *Villanova Law Review*, 1993, 38, 487–514.

Kaplan, C. S. "Suit Against Cornell Dropped in International Libel Case." *Cyberlaw Journal*, <www.nytimes.com/library/tech/98/11/cyber/cyberlaw/06law.html>, Jun. 21, 1999.

Kaplin, W. A. and Lee, B. A. *A Legal Guide for Student Affairs Professionals.* San Francisco, CA: Jossey-Bass Publishers, 1997, 342.

Katsh, M. E. "Dispute Resolution in Cyberspace." *Connecticut Law Review*, Summer 1996, 28, 953–980.

Kiernan, V. "3 Universities in California Find Themselves Linked to Hacker Attacks." *Chronicle of Higher Education*, Feb. 25, 2000, A51.

Mangan, K. S. "Anonymous E-Mail Message at Stanford U. Law School Ignites Debate Over Free Speech." *Chronicle of Higher Education*, <chronicle.com/daily/99/02/99022205n.htm>, Feb. 22, 1999.

McDonald, S. J. "Whose Computer Is It, Anyway?" Paper presented at the 20th annual national conference of Stetson University College of Law on Law and Higher Education, Feb. 11–13, 1999.

McGraw, D. K. "Sexual Harassment in Cyberspace: The Problem of Unwelcome E-Mail." *Rutgers Computer and Technology Law Journal*, 1995, 20, 491–518.

Monaghan, P. "A Dispute Over a Professor's E-Mail Illustrates the Complexities of Acceptable Use Policies." *Chronicle of Higher Education*, Mar. 9, 1999, A25.

Nimmer, M. B. *Nimmer on Copyright*. New York: Matthew Bender, 1993.

Oldenkamp, E. "Pornography, the Internet, and Student-to-Student Harassment: A Dilemma Solved with Title VII and Title IX." *Duke Journal of Gender Law and Policy*, 1997, 4, 159–179.

Olsen, F. "Any Computer Can Be a Launching Pad for Hackers, Security Expert Warns." *Chronicle of Higher Education*, Jan. 21, 2000, A42.

Olsen, F. "Do 'Digital Certificates' Hold the Key to Colleges' On-Line Activities?" *Chronicle of Higher Education*, Dec. 10, 1999, A47.

O'Neil, R. M. "The Internet in the College Community." *Northern Illinois University Law Review*, 1997, 17, 191–203.

Pavela, G. "Electronic Communications on Campus." *SYNTHESIS: Law and Policy in Higher Education*, Spring 1996, 7, 546.

Post, D. "Dispute Resolution in Cyberspace: Engineering a Virtual Magistrate System." <www.law.vill.edu/ncair/disres/DGP2.HTM>, Apr. 1, 1999.

Price, J. R. "College and Universities as Internet Service Providers: Determining and Limiting Copyright Infringement." *Journal of College and University Law*, 1996, 23, 183–229.

Prosser, W. L. *The Handbook of the Law of Torts*. St. Paul, Minn.: West Publishing Co., 1971.

Restatement of the Law, Second-Torts. St. Paul, Minn.: American Law Institute, 1977.

Restatement of the Law, Second-Conflict of Laws. St. Paul, Minn.: American Law Institute, 1971.

Rimm, M. "Marketing Pornography on the Information Superhighway: A Survey of 917, 410 Images, Descriptions, Short Stories, and Animations Downloaded 8.5 Million Times by Consumers in Over 2000 Cities in Forty Countries, Provinces, and Territories." *Georgetown Law Journal*, 1995, 83, 1849–1926.

Sergent, R. S. "A Fourth Amendment Model for Computer Networks and Data Privacy." *Virginia Law Review*, 1995, 81, 1181–1205.

Simon, T. S. "Faculty Writing: Are They Works for Hire under the 1976 Copyright Act?" *Journal of College and University Law*, 1982, 9, 485–513.

Smiddy, L. O. "Choosing the Law and Forum for Litigation of Disputes." in *Toward a Law of Global Communications Networks*, ed. A. W. Branscomb, New York, NY: Longman, 1986, 303.

Tedford, T. L. *Freedom of Speech in the United States*. New York: McGraw-Hill, 1993.

Templeton, B. "Linking Rights." <www.templetons.com/brad/linkright.html>, Mar. 19, 2000.

Tenenbaum, J. S. "Associations Immunized from Liability for Member's E-Mail." *The Internet Newsletter Business and Legal Aspects*, Mar. 1998, 10.

Thompson, C. "Turning College Names into a Business." *Cybertimes*, <www.nytimes.com/library/cyber/week/1103name.html>, Nov. 3, 1996.

Weiner, S. H. "Report: A Lawyer's Ramble Down the Information Superhighway: Forum Non Conveniens." *Fordham Law Review*, Dec. 1995, 64, 845–850.

Zaphiriou, G. A. "Basis of the Conflict of Laws: Fairness and Effectiveness." *George Mason University Law Review*, Spring 1988, 10, 301–326.

Zebrak, S. A. "A Step-by-Step Guide to Handling Domain Name Disputes." *The Computer Lawyer*, Apr. 1999, 16, 21–26.

"Note: The Privacy Act of 1974: An Overview and Critique." *Washington Law Quarterly*, 1976, 667–670.

Case Index

Index